中國成語選粹新篇

編 者
盧 榮 軒

英譯者
孫 利 傑

插 圖
李 士 伋

和平圖書・海峰出版社

BEST CHINESE IDIOMS

(Volume 3)

Compiled by

LO WING HUEN

Tr. into English by

SUN LI JIE

Illustrated by

LI SHI JI

Peace Book • Hai Feng Publishing Co.

ISBN 962-238-248-7
HF-269-P

BEST CHINESE IDIOMS (Volume 3)

Compiled by	Lo Wing Huen
Tr. into English by	Sun Li Jie
Illustrated by	Li Shi Ji
Edited by	Irene Li
Art designed by	Ki-Coo Seto
Published by	HAI FENG PUBLISHING COMPANY Rm. 1502 Wing On House, 71 Des Voeux Road Central, Hong Kong
Printed by	FRIENDLY PRINTING COMPANY LTD. Flat B1, 3/F., Luen Ming Hing Ind. Bldg., 36 Muk Cheong St., Tokwawan, Kowloon, H.K.
Format	142 x 210 mm
Edition	First Edition July 1997

中國成語選粹新篇

編者	盧榮軒
英譯者	孫利傑
插圖	李士伋
責任編輯	李月薇
裝幀設計	司徒綺雲
出版	海峰出版社 香港中環德輔道中 71 號永安集團大廈 1502 室
印刷	友利印刷有限公司 九龍土瓜灣木廠街 36 號聯明興工業大廈四樓 B1 座
規格	(大 32 開) 142 x 210 mm
版次	一九九七年七月第一版

Published & Printed in Hong Kong

前言

漢語有豐富的詞匯和各種形式的固定詞組。成語就是一種經常使用的固定詞組，在漢語詞匯中佔有重要的地位。

漢語成語形式簡潔、含義深刻。它們常被用來說明一件事實、一個道理或比喻一種形象，從而構成漢語的獨特風格。

漢語成語是在漢語的長期發展過程中形成的。大多數成語由四個字組成，在使用的時候實際上相當於一個詞。在談話、演講或寫作時，如運用得當，將會增強語言的感染力，產生其他方法所不能比擬的表達效果。

正確地運用成語，首要之點在於瞭解它的意義。有些成語的意義，從字面上不難瞭解；有些成語則不能按字面望文生義，而必須知道它的來源，才能準確掌握和運用。

漢語成語，數量龐大，除來自民間口語者外，相當大的部分來自古代典籍。這些來自古代典籍的成語，有的出自寓言故事，有的出自歷史事件或神話傳說，通常也叫典故。本書所選的大都屬於這一類。

中國的古代典籍記載了大量絢麗多彩的寓言故事和神話。這在先秦諸子的著作中尤為顯著，其中許多寓言故事和神話都有成語的概括形式，如“畏影惡跡”（參見第一八四頁）、“鷗鳥不下”（參見第二六八頁）。歷史上的事件，也常常被概括為一個成語，如“雁足傳書”（參見第二一九頁）、“四分五裂”（參見第八十二頁）。這些來自寓言、神話和歷史事件的成語，有不少蘊含著深刻的哲理和寶貴的生活經驗，直到今天還有其現實意義。此外，還有一些成語，來源於古代作品中的名句，因而成了格言。

本書為一九八四年出版的《中國成語選粹》和一九八八年出版的《中國成語選粹續篇》的新篇，共收錄常用的和有故事性的成語一百九十七條。在介紹成語故事時，為使讀者容易瞭解起見，有的地方作了一些刪節和修飾，增加了一點背景材料。許多中國成語並列有意義相近的英語成語。此外，還在成語條目的下面附加漢語拼音，不懂漢語的讀者，可以借助於"漢語拼音發音指南"（見書後），直接讀出漢語成語。

書前成語"目次"按首字筆劃順序排列。書末附有"英文索引"和按漢語拼音字母順序排列的"漢語拼音索引"。

FOREWORD

The Chinese language is rich in vocabulary, phrases and idioms. As a form of set phrases, Chinese idioms are in wide use and occupy an important place in the language as a whole. Concise yet meaningful, they illustrate certain specific facts, carry certain moral teachings or suggest certain particular images, thus constituting a unique characteristic of the Chinese language.

Chinese idioms, which emerged and developed in the long years of Chinese history, mostly consist of four characters which go together and virtually function as a set term. When used properly and cleverly in everyday conversation, speeches or writings, they add to the appeal of the language and make it more to the point and achieve what cannot be achieved by other ways of expressing the same thought.

A correct understanding of their meaning is the key to the correct use of Chinese idioms. While some can be taken literally, others cannot be interpreted or used correctly without first delving into their real meaning and origin.

Being numerous and having backgrounds that can be traced back to ancient times, Chinese idioms are partly derived from oral language and partly — perhaps in the case of a greater percentage of them — from ancient historical records, literature and other writings. The latter category, with which this book chiefly deals, embraces those coming from parables or fables, historical stories or anecdotes, and fairy tales or legends.

Chinese historical records of the remote past abound in wise fables, didactic parables and thought-provoking tales. A case in point is the works of the philosophers of the various schools prior to the Qin Dynasty (221-207 B.C.). Many of the fables and tales contained in them are summarized in a few words, such as "Scared of His Own Shadow, and Detesting His Own Footprints" (see P.184 of this book) and "The

Seagulls Won't Come Down" (see P.269). Some idioms deal with historical events or anecdotes, such as "Wild Geese Deliver Letters" (see P.219) and "Break into Four Parts, and Each Part Cracks into Five Pieces" (see P.82). Quite a number of Chinese idioms belonging to the above categories carry a philosophical note and draw on practical experiences, which make them significant even for contemporary life. There are also some idioms which have been taken from well-known ancient works and have thus become maxims.

The present book, a new chapter of *Best Chinese Idioms* published in 1984 and *Best Chinese Idioms* (Volume 2) published in 1988, contain 197 Chinese idioms which are in common use and behind each of which there is a story or an anecdote. Generally speaking, the stories and anecdotes are based on the original versions in classical Chinese but, where necessary, abridgement and modifications are made and brief descriptions of their backgrounds given. Many of the Chinese idioms are accompanied by English equivalents. Chinese phonetic spelling (*pinyin*) is given to each title, and for readers who are not familiar with this system the appendix "Guide to Chinese Phonetic Alphabet" at the end of the book may prove useful.

The table of contents in this book has been arranged according to the number of strokes of the first Chinese character in each title. There is an English Index and a Chinese Phonetic Alphabet Index compiled alphabetically, using the *pinyin* system at the end of the book.

目次
CONTENTS

一往情深 23
Cherishing a Deep-seated Affection
一去不復返 24
Once Gone, It Never Comes Back
一目十行 25
Reading Ten Lines at a Glance
一不做，二不休 26
Once It Is Started, Go through with It
一場春夢 28
A Spring Dream
一國三公 29
Three Sovereigns in One Country
一動不如一靜 30
Better to Keep Still Than Move
一簞一瓢 31
A Basket of Rice, a Gourd Dipper of Drink
一網打盡 33
Capturing All in One Net
二桃殺三士 34
Killing Three People with Two Peaches
八仙過海，各顯神通 36
Eight Immortals Cross the Sea, Each One Showing His or Her Special Prowess
九牛一毛 38
A Single Hair Out of Nine Ox Hides

九轉功成 40
Success After Nine Conversions
人死留名 41
Leaving a Name Behind
人面桃花 42
Her Face Is Like a Peach Blossom
人面獸心 44
A Human Face with the Heart of a Beast
人為刀俎，我為魚肉 45
Like Fish or Meat on a Chopping Board
入幕之賓 46
A Guest Behind the Curtain
力不從心 48
Strength Not Equal to the Will
三教九流 49
The Three Religions and Nine Schools
三姑六婆 50
Three Nuns and Six Old Women
三紙無驢 51
No Mention of Donkey on Three Pages
大筆如椽 52
Rafter-like Writing Brush
千里之堤，潰於蟻穴 53
One Anthill May Cause the Collapse of a Thousand-Li Dyke
下車泣罪 54
Alighting from the Carriage and Weeping over One's Misdeed
下筆成章 55
Writing a Composition in a Stream
小時了了，大未必佳 57
A Clever Child May Not Distinguish Himself When Grown

之乎者也 58
Zhi-Hu-Zhe-Ye
天馬行空 59
A Heavenly Steed Soaring Across the Skies
天下第一 60
The First Under Heaven
不可救藥 61
Too Far Gone To Be Remedied
不遺餘力 63
Sparing No Pains
不可同日而語 64
Not To Be Mentioned in the Same Breath
不辨菽麥 66
Unable to Tell Beans from Wheat
不學無術 67
No Study, Know Nothing
什襲珍藏 69
Wrapping a Treasure Up Layer by Layer for Storage
千變萬化 70
One Thousand Changes and Ten Thousand Transformations
升堂入室 72
Passing Through the Hall into the Inner Chamber
牛角掛書 73
Hanging a Book on an Ox Horn
文武之道，一張一弛 74
The Principle of Kings Wen and Wu Was to Alternate Tension with Relaxation
以人為鑒 75
Using Others as Mirrors
以火救火，以水救水 76
Fighting a Conflagration with Fire and Controling a Flood with Water

以管窺天 77
Looking at the Heavens Through a Tube
以貌取人 78
Judging a Person Solely by His Appearance
以酒解醒 80
Drinking More to Cure Drunkenness
太歲頭上動土 81
Breaking Ground Where the God of the Year Presides
四分五裂 82
Break into Four Parts, and Each Part Cracks into Five Pieces
四海之內皆兄弟 83
All Men Are Brothers Within the Four Seas
目不見睫 85
The Eye Cannot See Its Lashes
白雲親舍 86
Parents Living Under the White Clouds
付諸洪喬 87
Putting Letters in Hongqiao's Charge
立於不敗之地 88
Establishing Oneself in an Unassailable Position
出言不遜 89
Making Impertinent Remarks
平易近人 90
Amiable and Easy to Approach
汗牛充棟 92
Enough Books to Make a Pack-Ox Sweat Or to Pile Ceiling-High
汗流浹背 93
Sweat Streaming Down and Drenching One's Back
羊左之交 94
Friendship Between Yang Jiaoai and Zuo Botao

米珠薪桂 95
Rice as Precious as Pearls and Firewood as Costly as Cassia
安於故俗，溺於舊聞 96
Satisfied with Old Customs and Outdated Information
老嫗能解 97
Intelligible to an Old Woman
死不瞑目 98
Dying Without Closing One's Eyes
百折不撓 100
Never Bending in Spite of Repeated Twisting
有志者事竟成 102
A Man with a Set Purpose Will Finally Succeed
有名無實 103
In Name but Not in Reality
行不得也哥哥 104
The Road Is Hard and We Can't Go On
(Xing-Bu-De-Ye-Ge-Ge)
全無心肝 105
Totally Heartless
羽毛未豐 107
The Feather Is Not Yet Fully Grown
回天之力 108
Power Capable of Drawing Back a Moving Heavenly Body
同甘共苦 109
Sharing Joy and Woe
先下手為強 111
He Who Strikes First Prevails
先入為主 112
First Impressions Are Strongest
先憂後樂 114
Be the First to Show Concern and the Last to Enjoy Oneself
先聲後實 115
Proclaiming One's Might First and Then Demonstrating It

先禮後兵 116
Courteous Before Resorting to Force
各得其所 118
Each in His Own Place
自慚形穢 119
Ashamed of One's Ungainly Appearance
好整以暇 120
Remaining Composed in Difficult Situations
如出一口 121
Uttered As If from One Mouth
朽木糞牆 122
Decayed Wood and Dirt Wall
沆瀣一氣 123
Hang and Xie Breathe the Same Breath
沐猴而冠 124
A Monkey Wearing a Hat
言不由衷 125
The Words Spoken Are Not from the Heart
初出茅廬 126
Just Coming out of the Thatched Cottage
求仁得仁 128
Seeking Benevolence and Acquiring It
赤膊上陣 129
Going into Battle Stripped to the Waist
攻心為上 130
Attacking the Enemy's Mind Is the Most Important of All
吾道東矣 131
My Theory Has Been Transmitted to the East
見利忘義 132
Disregarding Moral Principles in Pursuit of Profit
防民之口，甚於防川 134
Stopping People's Mouths Is More Difficult Than Damming Rivers

吳下阿蒙 135
Lu Meng in the Kingdom of Wu
別開生面 136
Opening Up a Fresh Look
坐山觀虎鬥 137
Sitting on Top of the Mountain to Watch the Tigers Fight
坐懷不亂 138
Not Disturbed with a Pretty Woman in One's Lap
兵不厭詐 140
Nothing Is Too Deceitful in War
兵貴神速 141
Speed Is What Counts in War
我醉欲眠 143
I Am Drunk and Want to Sleep
我見猶憐 144
When I See Her, Even I Cannot Help Loving Her
改過自新 145
Correct One's Errors and Start Anew
長袖善舞 146
Skillful at Dancing with Long Sleeves
沾沾自喜 148
Being Pleased with Oneself
兩袖清風 149
Two Sleeves Flapping in the Wind
盲人瞎馬 151
A Blind Man on a Blind Horse
青雲直上 152
Soaring High into the Clouds
金屋藏嬌 154
Keeping Ah Jiao in a Chamber of Gold
金剛怒目 155
Glaring Like a Vajra

狐死首丘 156
A Fox Dies with Its Face Toward Its Den
枕戈待旦 157
Sleep on One's Spear Till Daybreak
杵臼之交 158
Making Friends by the Pestle and Mortar
杳如黃鶴 159
Disappearing Like the Yellow Crane
披荊斬棘 160
Hacking Through Brambles and Thistles
抱殘守缺 161
Clinging to the Broken and Outworn
居安思危 162
Think of Danger While Living in Peace
明鏡高懸 163
A Bright Mirror Hanging High
首尾相應 165
Head and Tail Correspond with Each Other
神機妙算 166
Clever Strategy and Shrewd Tactics
神龍見首不見尾 168
The Head of the Magic Dragon Is Visible and Its Tail Invisible
亭亭玉立 169
Standing Gracefully Erect
枯樹生花 170
A Withered Tree Brings Forth Flowers
相提並論 171
Mentioned in the Same Breath
相生相克 172
Reinforcing and Counteracting Each Other
南山可移，判不可搖 173
Mt. Zhongnan Might Be Removed, But the Decision

Might Not Be Removed
風吹草動 174
The Grass Stirs When the Wind Blows
信口雌黃 176
Loosening One's Tongue and Using Orpiment Freely
後生可畏 177
The After-Born Should Be Regarded with Awe
飛短流長 178
Rumors and Gossip Travel Apace
飛將數奇 180
The Winged General Has a Bad Fortune
羿射九日 181
Yi Shoots Down Nine Suns
韋編三絕 183
The Bookbinding Snaps Three Times
畏影惡跡 184
Scared of His Own Shadow, and Detesting His Own Footprints
旁若無人 185
Acting As If There Were No One Near
剖腹藏珠 186
Cutting One's Belly Open to Hide a Pearl
唐突西施 187
Offending Xi Shi the Beauty
狼狽為奸 188
Wolf and Bei Jackal in Cahoots with Each Other
徒有虛名 189
Existing in Name Only
乘風破浪 191
Riding the Wind and Breaking the Waves
乘興而來 192
Coming While in a Joyful Mood

捉刀人 193
The Man Holding a Sword
氣殺鍾馗 194
Zhong Kui Dies of Indignation
烏合之眾 196
A Crowd Assembling Like Crows
流連忘返 197
So Lost in Enjoyment As to Forget to Go Home
莫須有 198
It Might Be True
莫躓於山，而躓於垤 200
Stumbled by a Mound Instead of a Mountain
剛愎自用 202
Headstrong and Opinionated
殺彘教子 203
Killing the Pig to Teach the Child
卿卿我我 204
Qing-Qing-Wo-Wo
魚目混珠 205
Passing Off Fish Eyes As Pearls
假途滅虢 207
Borrowing a Road to Conquer the State of Guo
黃袍加身 207
Draped with the Imperial Yellow Robe
萬死不辭 208
Not to Be Daunted by Ten Thousand Deaths
萬里長城 210
The Great Wall
捨命陪君子 211
I Would Throw My Lot in with You, Sir, at the Risk of My Life
掃榻以迎 212
Sweeping the Bed Clean in Expectation of a Visitor

割蓆斷交 213
Cutting the Mat to Break with an Old Friend
終南捷徑 214
A Short Cut in Mount Zhongnan
強不知以為知 215
Making a Pretense of Knowledge
善自為謀 216
Knowing How to Look After Oneself
超群絕倫 217
Far Above the Ordinary
雁足傳書 219
Wild Geese Deliver Letters
虛有其表 220
Looking Impressive but Lacking Real Worth
期期艾艾 221
Qi-Qi-Ai-Ai
紫氣東來 222
The Purple Air Comes from the East
極樂世界 224
Western Paradise
貽笑大方 225
Exposing Oneself to Ridicule by the Knowledgeable
董狐直筆 226
Dong Hu's Straight Writing Brush
過門不入 227
Passing One's Own House but Never Going In
解鈴還須繫鈴人 228
Better Let Him Who Tied the Bell Untie It
盡忠報國 230
Serving One's Country Loyally
豎子成名 231
That Fellow Has Made His Name

漸入佳境 233
Gradually Entering Blissful Circumstances
撥雲見日 234
Dispelling the Clouds and Seeing the Sun
綠衣使者 235
The Messenger in Green
綠葉成陰 236
Green Leaves Make a Shade
銅山西崩，洛鐘東應 238
Tongshan Mountain Falls in the West and Luo Bronze Bell Responds in the East
嘔心瀝血 239
To Vomit Out the Heart and Drip Blood
暮夜無知 240
No One Knows in the Dead of the Night
撲朔迷離 242
Feet Kicking and Eyes Narrowed
談笑自若 243
Talking and Laughing As If Nothing Had Happened
賣刀買牛 245
Selling the Knife to Buy Cattle
戮力同心 246
Pulling Together and Working with One Heart and One Mind
黎丘丈人 247
The Old Man at Liqiu
銷聲匿跡 248
Keep Silent and Vanish Without Leaving a Trace Behind
舉棋不定 250
Hesitate at Making a Chess Move
獨當一面 252
Taking Sole Charge on Any Battlefront

澠池之功 253
Rendering Meritorious Service at Mianchi
錢可通神 255
Money Can Move Even the Gods
鬨堂大笑 256
Setting the Whole Room Roaring
縱橫捭闔 257
Lengthwise and Breadthwise, Opening and Closing
斷頭將軍 259
A General Who Fears Not the Loss of His Head
斷鶴續鳧 260
Shortening the Leg of a Crane to Lengthen the Leg of a Wild Duck
藍田生玉 261
Jade Produced in Lantian
藥籠中物 263
Things in the Medicine Kit
寵辱不驚 264
Not Moved by Honor or Disgrace
懸駝就石 265
Hanging the Camel up to Be Near to the Whetstone
響遏行雲 266
The Music Stops the Passing Clouds
顧名思義 267
Thinking What a Title or Name Implies
鷗鳥不下 268
The Seagulls Won't Come Down
囊螢映雪 269
Bagged Fireflies and the Reflected Light of the Snow

一往情深

yī wǎng qíng shēn

一如既往，情深似海；對人或事物一直有深摯、濃厚的感情。

東晉將軍桓伊，英勇善戰，為東晉的江山立下了不少戰功。桓伊為人正直，謙遜有禮，雖然戰績顯赫，卻從不居功自傲。他很喜愛音樂，尤擅長吹笛；他也很喜歡聽人唱歌，每當聽到妙曼之處，就情不自禁地陶醉在音樂的世界裡。宰相謝安說："桓伊對音樂的感情是發自內心，真可謂'一往有深情'。"

出自《世說新語》

Cherishing a Deep-seated Affection

Said of people who are passionately and consistently devoted to somebody or something.

Huan Yi, a general of the Eastern Jin Dynasty, was brave and sagacious in battle and performed many military exploits for the empire. He was an honest and modest person and never prided himself on his merits. He loved music very much and was good at playing the flute. While listening to beautiful songs, he was unable to restrain his emotions and often felt enchanted by the magic of music. Xie An, the prime minister at that time, once said that Huan Yi's love for music was deep-seated and came from the bottom of his heart.

New Social Anecdotes

一去不復返

yī qù bù fù fǎn

一旦去了再不回來；比喻過去了的事情，似水流年不回頭。

戰國末期，國力強大的秦國威脅著各國。燕太子和勇士荊軻謀劃刺殺秦王，為取得秦王的信任，太子丹把秦王的仇人樊於期的首級和燕國的地圖交給荊軻假意獻給秦王，伺機刺殺。

荊軻動身赴秦，太子丹眾人都穿著素白衣冠到易水邊為荊軻餞行，荊軻壯懷激烈，慷慨高歌："風蕭蕭兮易水寒，壯士一去兮不復還！"眾人聽了都不禁垂淚涕泣。

出自《史記》

一去不復返

Once Gone, It Never Comes Back

Used in reference to things or times that have passed and will never return.

At the end of the Warring States Period, the powerful Qin was a great menace to the other states. Dan, the heir-apparent of the Yan State, and warrior Jing Ke planned to assassinate the king of Qin. To win the trust of the king of Qin, Dan asked Jing Ke to present the severed head of Fan Yuqi, the enemy of the king of Qin, and a map of Yan to the king as a gift, and watch for a chance to kill him.

On Jing Ke's departure for Qin, Dan and others, all dressed in white, went to the Yishui River to say farewell to him. Jing Ke sang a song excitedly and fervently, "Biting is the wind and cold the river, I will come back never forever!" All the people broke into tears while hearing the song.

Records of the Historian

一目十行

yī mù shí háng

一眼就可看十行字；形容閱讀速度很快。

南北朝時期，梁武帝蕭衍的兒子蕭綱小時候已非常聰穎，六歲就會寫詩作文。梁武帝對他悉心栽培，並且期望他到七歲時的文章才華可以和七步成詩的曹植相比。蕭綱長大後，讀書的興趣越發濃厚。他博覽群書，諸子百家無一不曉。讀書時，往往一眼就看十行，速度非常快。梁武帝死後，蕭綱繼位稱為簡文帝。

出自《梁書》

Reading Ten Lines at a Glance

Said of speed reading.

During the Southern and Northern Dynasties, Xiao Yan, known as Emperor Wudi of the Liang Dynasty, had a very smart son named Xiao Gang who could compose poems and write essays at the age of six. The emperor taught Xiao Gang many things and hoped that when he was seven his talent could be compared with Cao Zhi, who could compose a poem in the time required for taking seven steps. By the time Xiao Gang had grown up, he had read all the works written by the great thinkers of the numerous schools of the late Zhou Dynasty. He could read rapidly, covering ten lines with a single glance. Upon the death of his father, Xiao Gang succeeded to the throne and was called Emperor Jianwen.

History of the Liang Dynasty

一不做，二不休

yī bù zuò, èr bù xiū

一是不做，二是做了就不要停止；意思是不做則已，一做就做到底。

唐德宗年間，張光晟追隨朱泚叛變，唐德宗派李晟領兵征討朱泚。在朱泚被困處於危局時，張光晟眼看朱泚快要失敗，於是便殺了朱泚，投降了李晟，以為這樣便可以脫身，免於死罪，但唐德宗還是把張光晟處了死刑。張光晟臨死前時說：“傳語後人：‘第一莫作，第二莫休’。”

出自《奉天錄》

Once It Is Started, Go through with It

Meaning a thing once begun should not be put off until done.

During the Tang Dynasty, Zhu Ci together with Zhang Guangsheng raised a rebellion. Emperor Dezong sent soldiers led by Li Sheng to punish them. When Zhu Ci was close to defeat, Zhang Guangsheng killed him and surrendered to Li Sheng. He thought that by doing this he would be exempted from being put to death. However, he was executed nonetheless. Before he died he said, "Let it be told to posterity: 'Don't do this thing, or if it's once begun, go through with it.'"

Book of Paying Tribute to Heaven

一不做，二不休

一場春夢

yī cháng chūn mèng

一場春宵好夢；比喻世事無常，富貴興衰有如一夢，轉眼成空。

北宋文學家、書畫家蘇東坡，因反對王安石的新法，以作詩“謗訕朝廷”罪被貶。後來又任翰林學士侍讀、禮部尚書，但最終又被貶謫。

他在浙江昌化的時候，有一天，他背著大瓢，在田間小道上，一邊走著一邊唱著歌的時候，迎面遇見了一個七十多歲的老婆婆。老婆婆憐憫地說：“翰林昔日的富貴，只是一場春夢罷了。”蘇東坡聽後，黯然無語。

出自《侯鯖錄》

一場春夢

A Spring Dream

Said of the transience of great wealth and high position.

Su Dongpo was a celebrated man of letters and calligrapher of the Northern Song Dynasty. He objected to Wang Anshi's reform, and was banished from the court for writing opposing poems. Later, he resumed office first as Court Academician, and then as Minister of Rites. However, he was again removed from the court. At the time he was in Changhua in Zhejiang, he walked one day on a country path with a gourd ladle on his back while singing, and came across a grandma in her seventies. The grandma said to him with pity, "Your wealth and position as an academician in the past is only a dream in spring." Hearing the words, Su Dongpo was depressed and said nothing.

Notes by Zhao Lingzhi

一國三公

yì guó sān gōng

一個國家，三個君主；比喻政令不統一，使人無所適從。

春秋時期，晉國君主晉獻公派大夫士蘇，為晉公子重耳和夷吾在蒲地、屈地修築城池。夷吾嫌士蘇修得不堅固，就向晉獻公告了狀。晉獻公責問士蘇道："你為甚麼不把城池修牢固呢？"士蘇回答說："我聽人說，沒有原因而憂愁的人，憂愁一定會來；沒有戰事而修築城池，城池一定會被敵寇所利用。我奉命為二位公子築城，若築得不堅固，恐怕要負對君主不恭的罪名；若築得堅固，被敵寇所用，又要負對君主不忠的罪名。我一旦沒有了對君主的恭敬和忠誠，還怎麼為您辦事呢？"士蘇後來對人說："穿著狐皮的人紊亂得像茸毛，一個國家有三個君主，我適從誰好呢？"

出自《左傳》

Three Sovereigns in One Country

Meaning not knowing who to follow among several supreme rulers.

During the Spring and Autumn Period, Duke Xian, ruler of the Jin State, asked senior official Shi Su to build city walls for each of his sons Chong Er and Yi Wu at their fiefs of Pu and Qu. Yi Wu was not satisfied with his wall and complained to Duke Xian that the wall was not strong enough. Duke Xian called Shi Su to account, "Why didn't you make the wall strong?" Shi Su replied, "I've heard that if one worries for no reason, he may finally have something to really worry about. We built the wall at a time when there was no war going on, but eventually the wall could be used by our enemy. If the walls I built for the two young lords are not strong, I would be accused of being disrespectful to you; but if the walls are very strong, and are used by our enemy, then this would be disloyal to you. Without respect and loyalty to the sovereign, how can I serve Your Highness?" Later, Shi Su talked about this to one of his friends, "There are three overlords in the state, which one shall I follow?"

Zuo Qiuming's Chronicles

一動不如一靜

yī dòng bù rú yī jìng

多一事不如少一事，或不要多此一舉，自找麻煩。

宋孝宗有一次遊覽天竺及靈隱，有一名叫輝的僧人陪同。當宋孝宗看到飛來峰時，饒有興味的問輝：“既是飛來的，如何不飛去？”

輝回答說："一動不如一靜。"

出自《貴耳集》

Better to Keep Still Than Move

Meaning sometimes taking no action is better than taking one which may make matters far worse.

Once Emperor Xiaozong of the Song Dynasty went sightseeing to Lingyin Temple accompanied by a monk named Hui. When the emperor saw the Peak That Flew Here, he asked Hui amusedly, "So the mountain flew here; why doesn't it fly away?" Hui answered, "Better keep still than move."

Notes by Zhang Duanyi

一簞一瓢

yī dān yī piáo

一筐籮飯，一瓜瓢水；形容清寒儉樸的生活。

顏回是孔子三千弟子之中最得意的門生，孔子經常要學生以他為榜樣，以仁義道德的標準來修養自己。顏回的生活很困難，過著極其貧寒的日子。但顏回不以為苦，每天以讀書、聽課為樂，時刻以孔子的教誨修養自己。孔子常常感慨地說："顏回真是有德行的人，一筐籮飯，一瓜瓢水，就這麼過日子。他住在陋巷裡，誰也不堪受這樣的苦，顏回卻能安貧樂道。"

可惜顏回活到三十一歲就早逝了，年逾花甲的孔子為失去心愛的學生而悲慟不已。

出自《論語》

A Basket of Rice, a Gourd Dipper of Drink

A Contented Mind Is a Perpetual Feast

Said of being content with frugal living.

Among Confucius' three thousand disciples, Yan Hui was his favorite. Confucius set him as an example for other students when they cultivated themselves in virtue and morality. Instead of complaining about his hard life, Yan Hui enjoyed reading and listening to Confucius' lessons every day and cultivated himself according to Confucius' teachings. Confucius was deeply moved and said, "Yan Hui is really a man of virtue. A basket of rice and a gourd dipper of drink are enough for him. Living in a shabby house that nobody could endure, he cares only for his principles and the Way."

Unfortunately, Yan Hui died when he was only thirty-one. Confucius, then in his sixties, was deeply grieved over losing his beloved student.

Confucian Analects

一網打盡

yī wǎng dǎ jìn

比喻一次就全部捕獲、消滅或一個不剩。

北宋時期，詩人蘇舜欽當了進奏院主官後，屢次上書，議論朝政得失，並且彈劾了宰相呂夷簡和御史劉元喻等人。呂夷簡等人含恨在心，伺機報復。有一次，蘇舜欽命人賣掉用過的公文封套，賣紙錢用來喝賽神酒，他自己也拿錢出來資助。劉元喻見機不可失，上書誣告蘇舜欽私賣公物，拿公家錢來喝酒，奢侈浪費。結果，蘇舜欽被皇帝撤職，連同所有參加酒會的人都受到處分。

大文學家歐陽修惋惜地說："想不到因為賽神酒會的事，一時俊傑的人都舉網而盡了。"

劉元喻陷害了蘇舜欽和他的朋友後，得意洋洋地說："我把他們這些人一網打盡了。"

出自《東軒筆錄》

一網打盡

Capturing All in One Net

Make a Clean Sweep

Said of catching all one's enemies and letting none escape.

During the Northern Song Dynasty, the poet Su Shunqin was appointed Chief of the Memorials Office. Several times he sent memorials to the emperor in which he expressed his views about running the state, and advocated the impeachment of Prime Minister Lu Yijian, Censor Liu Yuanyu, and others. Lu Yijian and Liu Yuanyu hated him very much and tried to find a way to retaliate. One day, Su Shunqin sold some used official document envelops and used the money to buy some liquor. Liu Yuanyu grasped this chance to get revenge and submitted a memorial in which he said Su Shunqin had sold public property without permission and used the money to hold a luxurious wine party. As a result, Su Shunqin was dismissed from his post and all the people who took part in the party also received punishment.

Ouyang Xiu, a great man of letters, said with pity, "To think that all the truly great men of our time should have been caught for attending a wine party!"

After the frame-up of Su Shunqin and his friends, Liu Yuanyu was quite pleased, "I have caught all my enemies in one net."

Handwritten Records on the Eastern Chamber

二桃殺三士

èr táo shā sān shì

用兩隻桃子殺了三人；比喻設計挑撥離間，借刀殺人。

春秋時，齊國的齊景公有三員猛將：公孫接、田開疆和古冶子。有一次，宰相晏嬰在路上遇見他們三人，他們對晏嬰不理不睬，毫不尊重。晏嬰非常生氣，就跑去對齊景公說："明君手下的將軍和官員，應懂君臣的禮節，守上下的規矩。可是公孫接、田開疆、古冶子三人，既無禮儀，又不守法規，不如趁早除去為上。"晏嬰獻上計謀："您送給他們三人兩隻桃子，讓他們論功而食。"

齊景公依計行事，他們三人收到桃子就爭吵起來。公孫接和田開疆搶先拿了桃子，古冶子見狀大怒，高叫著說："有一次，我護送君主過河時，君主的坐騎被河裡的大龜銜走了。是我潛水逆流而上一百步，再順流而下九里路，殺了大龜，救回了馬。論功勞我應該吃桃子，還我桃子！"說罷，拔劍而起。公孫接和田開疆感到羞愧，二人抽劍自刎而死。古冶子見二人自刎而死，以為因自己爭桃而迫死他們，頓時萬念俱灰，也一劍刺穿胸膛而亡。

出自《晏子春秋》

Killing Three People with Two Peaches

Said of sowing dissension among people, or trying to find an excuse to get rid of somebody.

During the Spring and Autumn Period, there were three valiant generals under Duke Jing of the Qi State, called Gongsun Jie, Tian Kaijiang, and Gu Yezi. Once, Prime Minister Yan Ying met the three generals on the street, but none of the three paid any heed to him. Yan Ying was very angry and said to Duke Jing, "Generals and officials under a wise sovereign should know how to observe the rules of protocol befitting their status. The three generals, Gongsun Jie, Tian Kaijiang, and Gu Yezi, have all failed to act up to the rules of proper conduct. We'd better get rid of them as soon as possible. Your Highness may give them two peaches, and ask them to take a peach according to their merits."

Duke Jing did what Yan Ying advised, and as expected, the three began to quarrel once they received the two peaches. Gongsun Jie and Tian Kaijiang picked the peaches first. Seeing this, Gu Yezi shouted at them furiously, "Once when I escorted our lord across the river a giant tortoise snatched our lord's horse away. It was I who went upstream for a hundred steps and then went downstream for 4.5 kilometers, finally killing the tortoise and saving the horse. I deserve one peach, give it back to me!" He then drew his sword. Gongsun Jie and Tian Kaijiang felt so much shame that they both two drew their swords and committed suicide. Gu Yezi thought it was he who forced them to death just for a peach. Plunged in grief and despair, he thrust his sword into his chest and killed himself.

Anecdotes of Yan Zi

八仙過海，各顯神通

bā xiān guò hǎi, gè xiǎn shén tōng

比喻人們在工作中，各自顯示能力、專長；也含有比試和競爭的意思。

鐵拐李、鍾離權、張果老、呂洞賓、藍采和、何仙姑、韓湘子和曹國舅，都是中國神話故事中家喻戶曉的人物。話說八仙參加完王母娘娘的壽宴，向王母娘娘告別，王母娘娘派五位美女送他們到雲端。他們接著要去參加龍華會，忽然看見腳下的東海白浪滔天，驚濤拍岸。

呂洞賓乘著酒興說：“我們駕雲飛過東海，顯不出仙家的本事，不如各投一物於水面，各顯神通渡海，如何？”眾仙大樂，齊聲說：“好！”紛紛投下寶物：鐵拐李的鐵拐、鍾離權的蒲扇、張果老的紙驢、呂洞賓的寶劍、韓湘子的簫管、何仙姑的花籃、藍采和的玉拍板、曹國舅的玉笏。眾仙站在寶物上破浪過海，巨浪驚人的東海面上好不熱鬧。這就是人們津津樂道的“八仙過海，各顯神通”的故事了。

出自《八仙出處東遊記傳》

Eight Immortals Cross the Sea, Each One Showing His or Her Special Prowess

Said of people trying to show their true worth and vying with each other.

Tieguai Li, Zhongli Quan, Zhang Guolao, Lu Dongbin, Lan Caihe, He Xiangu, Han Xiangzi, and Cao Guojiu are well-known figures in Chinese fairy tales. One day, when these eight immortals were going to leave the Queen Mother of the West Heaven's birthday banquet for the Dragon's Glory Ceremony, the Queen Mother sent five beauties to accompany them high in the clouds. On seeing the turbulent and raging waves of the East Sea under their feet, Lu Dongbin, on the strength of alcohol, said, "We can't show our true worth if we cross the sea by riding on clouds. How about each of us use his or her own talisman and we'll compete with each other?" The other immortals broke into laughter and said in one voice, "Good idea!" The eight immortals then threw their talismans in the sea—Tieguai Li's iron stick, Zhongli Quan's palm-leaf fan, Zhang Guolao's paper donkey, Lu Dongbin's magic sword, Han Xiangzi's bamboo flute, He Xiangu's flower basket, Lan Caihe's jade clappers, and Cao Guojiu's jade tablet. Standing on these talismans to cross the sea, the eight immortals made quite a sight.

The Eight Immortals' Voyage to the East

九牛一毛

jiǔ niú yī máo

九頭牛身上的一根毛；形容人或事物極其渺少輕微。

漢武帝派李陵領兵討伐匈奴，李陵一上陣就打了幾個勝仗，捷報傳來，漢武帝大悅。大臣們奉承皇帝，說皇帝知人善用；也讚李陵率軍有功。不久，李陵戰敗投降了匈奴，漢武帝盛怒。一些大臣為討好皇帝，反過來大罵李陵不忠、不義、無能。司馬遷力排眾議說李陵是一位英勇善戰的將軍，曾打過勝仗，殺敵一萬多。李陵以五千兵力之微，力敵匈奴八萬大軍，終因敵眾我寡，不得已才投降。李陵只是暫且偷生，將來報效朝廷。漢武帝聽了，龍顏震怒，把司馬遷關進大牢，並施用了極不人道的腐刑。司馬遷悲憤交加，想一死了之。後來他想通了，給好朋友任安的信寫道：“如果這樣死去，就像九頭牛的身上掉了一根毛，毫無意義，這與螻蛄、螞蟻有甚麼分別？”司馬遷忍辱負重，以頑強的意志和堅韌不拔的毅力，完成了不朽的歷史巨著《史記》。

出自《報任安書》

A Single Hair Out of Nine Ox Hides

A Drop in the Bucket

Used in reference to the insignificance of a man or a thing.

Emperor Wudi of the Han Dynasty sent an army led by Li Ling to suppress the Xiongnu tribe. At first, Li Ling won several battles, and the emperor was very happy at the news. The court officials flattered the emperor saying that he was wise for choosing a suitable general, and they also praised Li Ling's bravery. Before long, Li Ling was defeated and surrendered to the Xiongnus, and Emperor Wudi flew into a rage. In order to please the emperor, some court officials slandered Li Ling, saying he was disloyal, unrighteous, and incapable. However, Sima Qian said, "Li Ling is a brave general and has killed over ten thousand of the enemy in the battles he won. In the recent battle, fighting against Xiongnu's eighty thousand troops with only five thousand soldiers, he had no alternative but to surrender. He remains alive so he can contribute more to the country in the future." Furious at these words, Emperor Wudi put Sima Qian into jail and emasculated him. Torn between grief and indignation, Sima Qian thought of death. Later, he changed his mind. In his letter to Ren An, his good friend, he wrote, "If I kill myself now, my death is only one hair out of nine oxen. It's meaningless. Then what is the difference between my life and those of the crickets and ants?" Pocketing these insults, with a strong will and tenacious spirit, Sima Qian later finished his great historical work Records of the Historian.

Letters to Ren An

九牛一毛

九轉功成

jiǔ zhuǎn gōng chéng

經過九轉燒煉，終於功成；比喻經過反覆磨練，克服困難，終於大功告成。

據說道家修仙燒煉金丹，分為一轉至九轉，以九轉最為珍貴。燒煉金丹時，把丹砂燒成汞，再把汞燒煉成丹砂，如此循環燒煉。燒煉轉數少的金丹，藥力不夠，須要服用很長時間才能成仙；燒煉了九轉的金丹，功效顯著，短時間服用，很快就可以成仙了。

出自《抱朴子》

Success After Nine Conversions

Said of overcoming difficulties with repeated practice and finally achieving success.

It is said there are altogether nine conversions when the Taoists make pills of immortality, and the ninth conversion is the most important. Cinnabar is refined into mercury, and then the mercury is refined back into cinnabar. By this circulating refinement, the pill of immortality is made. When a person takes an immortality pill with fewer than nine conversions, it will take a long time for that person to become an immortal. If a person takes an immortality pill that has been made the right way, he will become an immortal in a short time.

The Book of Bao Pu Zi

人死留名

rén sǐ liú míng

人死後留名後世；生前建立功績，死後留美名於後世。

五代時，梁太祖朱溫死後，末帝朱友貞即位。末帝提升跟隨梁太祖轉戰多年的王彥章為濮州、澶州刺史。但末帝昏庸無道，朝中大事被奸臣把持，使王彥章不被重用，以致國土連連失地。

有一次，唐軍進攻梁朝，末帝不得不再重用王彥章。但這時強兵都已統屬奸臣段凝，只有五百御林軍給王彥章指揮，這些御林軍都是新召入伍的，沒幾天就敗下陣來，王彥章身負重傷，被唐軍俘擄了。

唐莊宗喜愛王彥章的驍勇善戰，勸他歸順。但王彥章說："我受梁的厚恩，哪有早上為梁朝做事，晚上為唐朝效力的呢？老百姓尚且說'豹死留皮，人死留名'，我今日一降，英名盡喪，還有甚麼面目見天下人？寧死不降，但求一死！"

出自《新五代史》

Leaving a Name Behind

Implying that when a man has made contributions, his name will be handed down to posterity.

During the Five Dynasties, Emperor Modi of the Later Liang Dynasty, known as Zhu Youzhen, succeeded to the throne upon the death of Emperor Taizu. Wang Yanzhang, who had followed Emperor Taizu to fight in the north and south, was promoted to prefect of Puzhou and Tanzhou by Emperor Modi. However, the emperor was incompetent and the state was ruled by evil officials. Wang Yanzhang remained in a lesser position, so the state's territory kept shrinking.

One day, the army of the Later Tang Dynasty launched an invasion against the Later Liang, and Emperor Modi had to once again ask Wang Yanzhang to fight against the enemy. At that time, all the crack troops were controlled by an evil official called Duan Ning. There were only five hundred palace guards, who were newly drafted, for Wang Yanzhang to command. Wang Yanzhang's army was defeated in a few days and Wang Yanzhang himself was badly wounded and was captured by the Later Tang army.

Emperor Zhuangzong of the Later Tang Dynasty, who had a high opinion of Wang Yanzhang for his bravery in battle, tried to persuade him to fight for the Tang army. However, Wang Yanzhang said to him, "I have received great kindness from Liang. How can I fight for Liang in the morning while fighting for Tang in the evening? People say, 'When a leopard dies, it leaves its skin behind; a man, his name.' If I surrender to you today, my name will go down as dirt in history. I would rather die than submit!"

New History of the Five Dynasties

人面桃花

rén miàn táo huā

內心傾慕而不能再見的女子；也形容景物依然，人事全非。

唐朝詩人崔護，有一年清明節的時候，他獨自到長安城南遊覽，看見一個宅院，於是敲門討水喝。崔護看見有一少女倚在小桃樹上，少女亭亭玉立，人比花美。崔護為之動心，一見傾情。

第二年的清明節，崔護又重訪城南郊外，以解相思之苦。可是桃花依舊，院門緊閉，再也見不到那可人兒。崔護傷感而發，在左邊的門扉上題了一首詩：“去年今日此門中，人面桃花相映紅。人面不知何處去，桃花依舊笑春風。”崔護題詩後，悵惘而去。

出自《本事詩》

人面桃花

Her Face Is Like a Peach Blossom

Said of a girl one loves but can't see anymore, or when affairs in life are greatly changed while the surroundings remain the same.

One year in early April, the Tang Dynasty poet Cui Hu went alone to visit south of Chang'an city. When he saw a house he knocked on the door and asked for something to drink. When the door opened, he saw a beautiful girl leaning against a young peach tree, with her charming face among the peach blossoms. Cui Hu fell in love with her at first sight.

The next year, again in early April, Cui Hu visited south of Chang'an again to alleviate the pain of his lovesickness. The peach blossoms were the same as before, but the door of the house was shut tightly and he didn't see his sweetheart again. Cui Hu was sad at heart and inscribed a poem on the left side of the door which said, "*Just inside this door the same day last year, A girl's face and the peach flowers reflected the glow of each other. Now the girl has gone somewhere I know not where, And the peach flowers are still in full bloom here.*" He then went away, despondent.

Narrative Poems

人面獸心

rén miàn shòu xīn

人的面貌，野獸的心腸；比喻外貌是人，內心卻像野獸般惡毒、卑鄙。

楊朱有一次在梁國遇上老子，他誠懇地向老子請教。老子講了這麼一個哲理：觀察人和事物，不要只看表面，應該看他的品德。聖人是重品德的，不會只看外表。人有身軀、手、足、頭髮、牙齒，外貌是人，但有些人的心卻是野獸的心腸；長有翅膀、有角、有爪、能飛、會跳的是飛禽走獸，可能有一顆善良的心。例如過去的伏羲氏、女媧氏、神農氏、夏后氏，全都是蛇身人面、牛頭虎鼻，沒有人的外貌，但他們卻有至高無上的聖德。所以我們看人主要是看他有沒有德行。

出自《列子》

A Human Face with the Heart of a Beast

Wolf in Sheep's Skin

Used in reference to someone who is a brute under a human mask.

Once Yang Zhu met Lao Zi in the state of Liang and he sincerely asked Lao Zi to teach him something. Lao Zi told him one truth: to evaluate someone, we should mainly judge from his morality instead of his exterior appearance. The sage highly valued virtue, but not appearances. Even with a torso, hands, feet, hair and teeth, one may have the heart of a beast. Those with wings, horns, and talons who can fly and jump are beasts, but they may have a kind heart. For example, Fu Xi, Nu Wa, Shen Nong, and Xia Hou have either a snake's body and a human's face or a bull's head and a tiger's nose, but they have superb virtue. Therefore, we should value only one's morality.

The Book of Lie Zi

人為刀俎，我為魚肉

rén wéi dāo zǔ, wǒ wéi yú ròu

別人是刀和砧板，我是魚和肉；被人掌握了生殺大權，自己處於被宰割的地位。

楚漢相爭時，項羽在咸陽城外的鴻門設下酒宴，邀請劉邦赴會；企圖在酒酣耳熱中，由項莊借舞劍助興為名，覓機刺殺劉邦，除去心腹之患。足智多謀的張良識破了項羽的陰謀，派樊噲保護劉邦。劉邦在酒宴上感應到殺機四伏，便遁詞上廁所溜走了。

劉邦心神不定地對樊噲說："我們不辭而別，這樣做可以嗎？"樊噲火急地說："哎呀，這個時候講究甚麼禮儀，人家把剁肉的用具都準備好了，就要把我們當魚，當肉吃了，告甚麼辭！"

出自《史記》

Like Fish or Meat on a Chopping Board

Said if one's fate is in the hands of others.

During the time when the Chu and Han kingdoms were fighting against each other, Xiang Yu, the king of Chu, set a banquet for Liu Bang, the king of Han, at Hongmen. Xiang Yu attempted to kill Liu Bang by asking one of his trusted generals, Xiang Zhuang, to perform a sword dance at the banquet. Zhang Liang saw through Xiang Yu's trick and assigned Fan Kuai to protect Liu Bang. Liu Bang sensed his dangerous situation and left the banquet on the pretext of going to the bathroom.

Uneasily, Liu Bang said to Fan Kuai, "Will it be against etiquette if we leave without saying goodbye?" Fan Kuai answered hurriedly, "How can you care about manners at a time like this? They have already prepared the chopping board and intend to kill us as meat and fish!"

Records of the Historian

入幕之賓

rù mù zhī bīn

進入幕帳的客人；指進入幕府參與機密大事的幕僚。

東晉時的郗超是一個博學廣聞的人，對天下大勢瞭如指掌。征西大將軍桓溫很賞識他的才智，請他當了參軍。桓溫是一個很主觀、很自信的人，輕易不會被人説服，但對郗超的見解卻言計聽從。

一天，司馬謝安到桓溫軍中商討國事。桓溫要郗超躲在軍帳幕後的床上，偷聽他們的談話。謝安和桓溫談意正濃之際，忽然一陣風吹入帳內，將帳幕吹起一角，郗超暴露了。桓溫覺得很不好意思，可謝安卻風趣地開玩笑説："郗超可真是入幕之賓啊！"謝安這一語相關的俏皮話，逗得大家哄笑起來。原來，郗超的字叫'喜賓'，'賓'的釋義就是客人的意思。

出自《晉書》

A Guest Behind the Curtain

Referring to someone serving as an advisor.

During the Eastern Jin Dynasty, there was a knowledgeable person named Xi Chao who knew state affairs like the palm of his own hand. General Huan Wen recognized Xi Chao's worth and asked him to be his advisor. Huan Wen was a man of self-confidence and could not be easily persuaded, but he always followed Xi Chao's advice.

One day, War Minister Xie An came to Huan Wen's place to discuss state affairs. Huan Wen asked Xi Chao to hide on the bed behind the curtain in his tent. While Xie An and Huan Wen were in heated discussion, there suddenly came a gust of wind and blew up a corner of the curtain. To Huan Wen's embarrassment, Xi Chao was exposed. Seeing this, Xie An joked, "Xi Chao is indeed your guest behind the curtain." Everyone laughed, because Xi Chao had another name—Xi Bin—of which "Bin" means "guest."

History of the Jin Dynasty

力不從心

lì bù cóng xīn

力量不能達到心願；形容能力不夠，不能實現願望。

東漢時的漢和帝劉肇，有一天收到一份來自邊疆西域的信函，拆開一看，原來是老將軍班超兄妹倆的奏章。奏章內述說了班超在西域征戰、鎮守已二十多年了，在漫長的軍旅生涯中，常常思念故鄉。現年已七十，體虛氣弱，鬢髮皆白，請求調回關內，頤養天年。班超的胞妹在奏章上寫道：“倘若西域突然發生暴亂，班超之氣力不能從心，有損國家基業……”漢和帝讀完奏章後，深受感動，親下詔書召班超回來。班超終於回到闊別三十一年的洛陽，不久，就病故了。

出自《後漢書》

Strength Not Equal to the Will

Bite Off More Than One Can Chew

Said if one's strength does not match one's ambitions.

One day during the Eastern Han Dynasty, Emperor Hedi received a letter from the Western Regions. He opened the letter and found it was a memorial written by an old general called Ban Chao and his younger sister. The letter said that having been assigned to guard the country's western frontier for over twenty years, Ban Chao missed his hometown very much, he was now in his seventies and was not in good health. So he asked to be recalled to his home where he would spend the rest of his days. Ban Chao's sister wrote in the letter, "If there were a riot in the Western Regions, and since Ban Chao is not strong enough to do as well as he would wish, it would do harm to the country's interests..." After he finished reading this memorial, Emperor Hedi was deeply moved and wrote an imperial edict recalling Ban Chao home. Finally, Ban Chao returned to his hometown of Luoyang after a long separation of thirty-one years. Not long after his return, Ban Chao died.

History of the Later Han Dynasty

力不從心

三教九流

sān jiào jiǔ liú

泛指宗教、學術領域中的各種學派；也比喻社會上各階層的人。

三教：儒教、道教、佛教。

九流：儒家、道家、陰陽家、法家、名家、墨家、縱橫家、雜家、農家。

出自《雲麓漫鈔》

The Three Religions and Nine Schools

Used in reference to various religious and academic sects and schools, or to people from all walks of life.

The three religions refer to Confucianism, Taoism, and Buddhism.

The nine schools are Confucianist, Taoist, Astrologist, Legalist, Logicist, Mohist, Diplomatist, Eclecticist, and Agriculturalist.

Notes by Zhao Yanwei

三姑六婆

sān gū liù pó

從事各種職業的女性；也貶指搬弄是非、無中生有的婦女。

三姑：尼姑、道姑、卦姑。

六婆：牙婆（買賣人口）、媒婆、師婆（女巫）、虔婆（鴇母）、藥婆、穩婆（接生婆）。

出自《輟耕錄》

Three Nuns and Six Old Women

Said of women of all professions, or women who tell tall tales and fabricate rumors.

The three nuns refer to nuns, Taoist nuns, and female fortune-tellers.

The six old women refer to female traders in human beings, female matchmakers, sorceresses, procuresses, female pharmacists, and midwives.

Notes Taken During Intervals of Ploughing in South Village

三紙無驢

sān zhǐ wú lǘ

譏諷文辭煩瑣，言不及義；或形容廢話連篇，離題萬丈。

從前有一個讀書人，經常吹噓自己博學多才，別人信以為真，尊稱他為‘博士’。有一天，博士買了一頭驢，付過錢後，要寫一張契約給賣驢人。博士為顯身手，提筆飛快地寫了三張紙才停筆。賣驢人説買頭驢子還要這麼複雜，博士聽了，不滿地説：“你懂甚麼！別人看了契約，一定會讚不絕口哩。”這時旁邊一個老人指著契約説：“怎麼三大張的契約上全然沒有一個‘驢’字的呢？！”博士聽了這話，羞得無地自容。

出自《顏氏家訓》

No Mention of Donkey on Three Pages

Used to deride writing crammed with empty verbiage and straying from the point.

Once upon a time there was a scholar who often boasted of his learning and talent. Other people took this as true and addressed him respectfully as "academician." One day, after sealing a deal with a trader for a donkey, the scholar was asked to write a voucher. In order to show off, the scholar dashed off three whole pages at one go. The trader began to complain about the lengthiness of the voucher and the scholar said unhappily, "You're so silly. Others will highly appreciate it!" An elder standing by pointed to the voucher and asked, "Why can't we find the single word of 'donkey' on any of these three pages?!" Hearing this, the scholar was too ashamed to utter a word.

Family Admonitions of the Yans

大筆如椽

dà bǐ rú chuán

大筆好像椽子（架著屋頂和瓦片的木條）；形容筆下有力，文章氣勢盛大。

東晉時的王珣，文思敏捷，下筆成章。有一天，他做了一個夢，夢見仙人送了一枝好像椽子那麼大的毛筆給他。夢醒後，他不時對人說將要寫很多文章。不久，皇帝死了。哀冊、謚議等的文章都由王珣起草。

出自《晉書》

Rafter-like Writing Brush

The writing brush here, compared to a rafter for its large size, is used in reference to a vigorous, powerful style of writing.

In the Eastern Jin Dynasty, there was a talented writer called Wang Xun. One day he dreamed that an immortal gave him a writing brush as big as a rafter. After that, he often told others that he would write many articles. This soon became true. After the emperor's death, it was Wang Xun who wrote the elegy and memorial articles.

History of the Jin Dynasty

千里之堤，潰於蟻穴

qiān lǐ zhī dī, kuì yú yǐ xué

千里的長堤因螞蟻洞而崩潰；比喻小過不改，將來會鑄成大錯。

古時候，有一個守護堤壩的人。有一天和朋友一同巡查堤壩，朋友偶然發現了堤上有一個螞蟻洞，提議趕緊堵塞蟻洞。但他不以為然，小小的螞蟻洞成不了氣候。

年復一年，螞蟻洞逐漸擴大了。洪水來臨時，在有螞蟻洞的地方都被洪水沖破了小洞，很快，小洞變成大洞。沒多久，長堤就崩潰了。

出自《韓非子》

One Anthill May Cause the Collapse of a Thousand-Li Dyke

A Stitch in Time Saves Nine

Said of a slight negligence that may lead to a great disaster.

One day in ancient times, when a guard was inspecting a dyke with his friend, an anthill was found by the friend. The friend advised the guard to stop up the hole immediately, but he didn't take it seriously, for he thought so small an anthill didn't matter.

As years went by, the anthill expanded gradually. When flood came, the places with anthills were washed into small holes. They quickly became large holes, and the long dyke finally collapsed.

The Book of Han Fei Zi

下車泣罪

xià chē qì zuì

下車對著罪犯落淚、哀傷；形容為政寬仁，愛民如子。

相傳禹因為治水有功，受到老百姓的愛戴和擁護；舜順應民心，讓出首領職位給禹。

有一天，禹坐車出去體察民情，在路上碰見幾個士兵押著一個犯人，禹馬上跳下車，拉著犯人的手瞭解案情。禹為犯人不守法紀的罪行而傷心落淚，士兵們想不通禹為甚麼哀傷。禹痛心地說："我雖然是首領，但我的心是與老百姓相連的，老百姓的苦難，我身同感受。

老百姓犯了罪，是我的過錯，是我對他們教化不好，因此我才悲傷啊！”

出自《説苑》

Alighting from the Carriage and Weeping over One's Misdeed

Said of a ruler applying a policy of benevolence and treating the people as beloved sons.

According to legend, Yu was venerated and supported by the people for his successful water control, so later Shun abdicated his throne to Yu.

One day, Yu went out by carriage to inspect the living conditions of the people. On his way he met a criminal escorted by several soldiers. Yu got off the carriage at once, held the criminal's hand, and asked about his case. Knowing the details, Yu began to weep. This puzzled the soldiers. Yu explained bitterly, "Though I'm the leader, my heart and the common people's beat as one. I count their sufferings as my own. It is my fault that they commit crimes, for I haven't tried my best to educate them. How can I hold back my tears!"

The Garden of Stories

下筆成章

xià bǐ chéng zhāng

一揮筆就寫成文章；形容才華橫溢，文思敏捷。

曹操的兒子曹植，自幼天資聰穎，喜愛詩辭歌賦。十幾歲就能背誦詩、論和辭賦數百篇，眾人都稱讚他是天生奇才。曹操心裡對兒子的才華頗為欣賞，但又似信非信。有一天，曹操隨意的問曹植：“你的文章我都看過了，寫得很好，不是別人代你寫的吧？”曹植趕忙跪下，稟告說：“我是言出為論，下筆成章，願意當面考試，我怎麼會請別人代寫文章的呢？”曹操聽了，哈哈大笑，對曹植更加寵愛了。

出自《三國志》

下筆成章

Writing a Composition in a Stream

Anything from his pen is already well-composed; alluding to one with superb writing talent and a quick mind.

Cao Zhi, Cao Cao's son, was born a prodigy. He loved poetry very much and could recite hundreds of verses, ditties, odes, and songs in his early teens, and he was praised as a genius. Cao Cao appreciated his son's talent at heart, but could hardly believe it. One day he said to Cao Zhi jokingly, "I have read your writings. They are well done, but I'm afraid they were written by others." Cao Zhi knelt down at once, and replied seriously, "I can finish an essay with a flourish of the pen. Why would I ask others to write for me? If you don't believe in me, you may give me a test right now!" Hearing this, Cao Cao laughed heartily. From then on, he loved Cao Zhi even more.

History of the Three Kingdoms

小時了了，大未必佳

xiǎo shí liǎo liǎo, dà wéi bì jiā

幼年時聰明伶俐，長大後未必成材。

東漢末期的文學家孔融，是建安七子之一。他十歲那年跟隨父親到洛陽。有一天，他去拜見李膺。他對李膺說："我和你本來就有親誼關係。"李膺覺得奇怪，問他說："你與我有甚麼關係呢？"孔融說："我的祖先孔仲尼（孔子）與你的先人李伯陽（老子）曾有師資之尊，所以我與你是世交通好哩。"李膺和賓客們見他口齒伶俐，活潑可愛，都十分欣賞他。只有陳韙不以為然，說："小時了了，大未必佳。"孔融應聲說："我想你小時，必當了了。"說得陳韙窘極了。

出自《世說新語》

A Clever Child May Not Distinguish Himself When Grown

Meaning it is not certain whether a smart child will grow up to be somebody.

Kong Rong, a writer in the late Eastern Han Dynasty, was one of the "Seven Great Scholars of the Jian'an Period." When he was ten years old, he went to Luoyang with his father. One day while paying a visit to Li Ying, he said to him, "We are kith and kin from our origin." Li Ying was surprised to hear that, and he asked, "But what's the relation between us?" Kong Rong said, "My ancestor Kong Zhongni (Confucius) was a pupil of your forefather Li Boyang (Master Lao Zi), so we are old family friends." Li Ying and his guests appreciated the boy's quick wit very much. But Chen Wei took a dim view of it. He said, "A clever child may not distinguish himself when grown." At these words, Kong Rong retorted, "I'm afraid you must have been very clever when you were young." Chen Wei was silenced embarrassingly.

New Social Anecdotes

之乎者也

zhī hū zhě yě

文言文裡的虛詞；諷刺喜歡咬文嚼字的人。

宋太祖趙匡胤，有一次巡視朱雀門，他指著寫上‘朱雀之門’的門額說：“為何不只寫‘朱雀門’，偏要加個‘之’字呢？”侍臣回答說：“這是‘語助’。”宋太祖哈哈大笑說：“‘之乎者也’助得甚麼？”

出自《湘山野錄》

Zhi-Hu-Zhe-Ye

Particles of classical Chinese; used to deride those who like to use archaisms.

Once when Zhao Kuangyin, the first emperor of the Song Dynasty, inspected "Zhu Que Men" (Scarlet Bird Gate), he pointed at the lintel with the four characters "Zhu Que Zhi Men" (Gate of the Scarlet Bird) and asked, "Why add the character 'Zhi' to 'Zhu Que Men'?" The attendant answered, "Because 'Zhi' is an auxiliary word." The emperor laughed and asked, "What auxiliary effect of Zhi can you find in 'Zhu-Que-Zhi-Men'?"

Random Notes by Wen Ying

天馬行空

tiān mǎ xíng kōng

神馬在天空中奔馳；形容才情俊逸，豪邁不羈。

漢武帝得自西域大宛國的優質馬，相傳日行千里；又叫‘西極天馬’、‘汗血寶馬’。

出自《薩天錫詩集》

A Heavenly Steed Soaring Across the Skies

Said of an unrestrained and vigorous writing style.

The fine horse of Emperor Wudi of the Han Dynasty, which was from the Dawan Kingdom of the Western Regions, was said to be able to gallop five hundred kilometers a day. So it was called "the Heavenly Horse from the West Extremes" and "Blood-Sweating Steed."

Poetry of Sa Tianxi

天下第一

tiān xià dì yī

普天下最好的一個；形容人或事物好得再沒有能相比的。

東漢大臣胡廣，少年時努力讀書，愛好寫詩，文學造詣不凡。

太守法雄的兒子法真推薦他考選拔試。試後，法真對父親說："胡廣這人品學兼優，應該推薦他去京師當官。"胡廣興奮地來到京師，將文章呈給了皇帝。東漢帝劉祜看完文章後，稱讚胡廣為天下第一。

胡廣進京不到三十天，皇帝就封他為尚書郎，後又升遷為尚書仆射。

出自《後漢書》

The First Under Heaven

The best in the world; said of unequalled persons or things.

Hu Guang, a minister of the Eastern Han Dynasty, studied very hard in his early youth. He had a great talent for literature, and was particularly fond of writing poems. Fa Zhen, son of the local governor Fa Xiong, recommended him to take the official selective examination. After the exam, Fa Zhen said to his father, "Hu Guang is a person of good moral character and fine scholarship, he should be recommended to fill an office in the capital." Then Hu Guang went to the capital excitedly, and submitted his writings to the emperor. The emperor, Liu Hu, praised him as the first under heaven after reading his writings, and appointed him Secretarial Court Gentleman within a month, and Vice-Director of the Imperial Secretariat not long after.

History of the Later Han Dynasty

不可救藥

bù kě jiù yào

病重到沒有藥可以醫治；比喻人或事物壞到無法挽救的地步。

西周後期，周厲王實施暴政，征戰不休，以致民不聊生，老百姓已到不可忍的地步。老臣凡伯眼看政局危殆，力諫厲王，直言朝政弊端，勸周厲王修德政，挽救國家。周厲王理也不理，朝中一些奸臣藉此嘲笑攻擊凡伯。凡伯憤恨交加，寫了一首長詩抨擊昏君奸臣，詩中一節寫周厲王昏庸無道，權臣氣焰囂張，國家到此地步，直是不可救藥！

果然如凡伯的預料，西周爆發了‘國人暴動’，周厲王倉惶而逃，西周從此衰落了。

出自《詩經》

不可救藥

Too Far Gone To Be Remedied

Too seriously ill to be cured; said of persons or things too far gone to be helped.

During the late years of the Western Zhou Dynasty, King Li's tyranny and incessant wars made life impossible for the people, and their patience finally came to the end. Worrying about the unstable political situation, the old court official Fan Bo remonstrated with the king over malpractices in the court administration and urged him to employ a benevolent rule to save the country. But King Li paid no attention to this, and it caused some treacherous court officials to ridicule and attack Fan Bo. Indignantly, Fan Bo wrote a long poem to impeach the muddle-headed king and treacherous officials, in which there was a stanza describing King Li's fatuity and the officials' arrogance, and pointing out that the situation in the country was too far gone to be remedied. As Fan Bo expected, riots soon broke out, and King Li fled from the capital in panic. The Western Zhou Dynasty waned from then on.

The Book of Songs

不遺餘力

bù yí yú lì

不惜剩餘的力量，無保留地用盡全部力量。

戰國時，有一次秦國攻打趙國，趙王召見大臣虞卿和樓昌，商量對策。

樓昌力主求和，虞卿反對求和。趙王說："秦這次不遺餘力，必定想攻陷趙國。"趙王害怕秦的強大，採用了樓昌的主張，派使者與秦國議和。可是秦兵趁機強攻猛打，圍困了趙國都邯鄲。秦國提出，趙國必須割讓六個城池方可議和。

頓時，趙國大臣分成兩派，一派主戰，一派主和。趙王沒了主意，這時，虞卿提出了一個計謀：六個城池不割讓秦國，贈給齊國，齊國得到好處，加上和秦國有仇，必然出兵攻秦，再聯合韓國和魏國，說不定秦國反過來要求和！

結果不出虞卿所料，秦國派使者來趙國講和了。

出自《史記》

Sparing No Pains

Leaving No Stone Unturned

Meaning sparing no effort to do one's level best.

During the Warring States Period, the Qin State once attacked the Zhao State. The king of Zhao called in the court officials Yu Qing and Lou Chang to ask for countermeasures. Lou Chang favored suing for peace, but Yu Qing objected to it. The king said, "It is obvious that Qin is going all out to destroy our state." Being afraid of the powerful Qin, the king adopted Lou Chang's proposal and sent a messenger to Qin to negotiate peace. But Qin seized the chance to besiege Handan, capital of Zhao. Qin said that only when Zhao ceded six cities to Qin could the peace treaty be made.

At once the court officials of Zhao fell into two groups, one was for fighting, the other against it. At that moment, Yu Qing proposed a scheme: giving the six cities to the Qi State instead of Qin. There was enmity between Qi and Qin, and when Qi profited, it was sure to attack Qin. Then Zhao would ally with Han and Wei. It is possible that then Qin would ask us for peace!

It happened just this way, and before long Qin sent a messenger to ask for peace.

Records of the Historian

不可同日而語

bù kě tóng rì ér yǔ

不可同一時間內談論；形容兩者相反或差異極大，不能相提並論。

戰國時候，蘇秦是合縱術的主張者。他主張燕、趙、韓、魏、齊、楚六國聯合，共同對付秦國。有一次，他來到趙國與趙王分析趙國的國力、地勢分佈和與鄰國相互屏障的地理環境。蘇秦說："六國的土地、軍力比秦國強大，如果六國合成一體，合力討伐秦國，秦國必敗無疑。可惜六國各自為政，只想著如何屈服秦國。打敗敵國和被敵國打敗，敵國當臣子和當敵國的臣子，這兩者豈可同日而語啊！"

趙王聽罷蘇秦的分析，封他為武安君，送他許多財帛，請他繼續游說其他國家。

出自《戰國策》

Not To Be Mentioned in the Same Breath

Said when great differences between two things or persons make them incomparable.

Su Qin was the advocate of the Vertical Theory. He advanced the idea that the Yan, Zhao, Han, Wei, Qi, and Chu states should be united against the Qin State. He went to Zhao and discussed that state's national strength and terrain with the king. Su Qin said that the combined territory of the six states was greater, and the military force more powerful than Qin, and that if the six states united to fight against it, Qin was sure to be defeated. He said it was a pity the six states each did things in its own way and thought only about submitting to Qin, when defeating the enemy or being defeated by the enemy couldn't be mentioned in the same breath!

Hearing Su Qin's views, the king made him Lord Wu'an, gave him much money and silk, and asked him to continue canvassing the other states.

Anecdotes of the Warring States

不辨菽麥

bù biàn shū mài

不能辨認豆和麥；形容愚昧無知或缺乏實際知識。

春秋時期，晉厲公驕奢淫逸，打獵時也把女人帶在身邊，一邊飲酒一邊狩獵，有些大夫對他的行徑十分不滿，他也想除掉不稱心的大夫。

有一天，晉厲公指使胥童、夷陽五、長魚矯率領武士包圍了郤錡、郤犫、郤至三人，並用長戈殺了他們。隨後，胥童在朝廷上劫持了欒書、中行偃，並想殺死他們。晉厲公阻止說："已殺了三個大夫，我不忍再殺人了，釋放他們，讓他們復職吧。"

欒書和中行偃僥倖保全了性命，思量著把晉厲公殺掉才是長久之計。有一次，晉厲公在匠麗氏那裡飲酒作樂，正興高彩烈間，欒書、中行偃突然襲擊逮捕了他。他們先後殺死了胥童、晉厲公等人，然後扶植晉襄公的後代周子當國君。周子這時只有十四歲，雖有一兄長，但愚昧無知，連菽麥都不能分辨出來，怎能立為國君？！周子即位後，稱為晉悼公。

出自《左傳》

Unable to Tell Beans from Wheat

Said of persons ignorant of practical matters.

During the Spring and Autumn Period, Duke Li of the Jin State led a luxurious and dissipated life. He always went hunting with women at his side, and drank liquor while hunting. Some court officials nursed a grievance over his behavior, and the king wanted to get rid of these troublesome officials. One day, he ordered Xu Tong, Yiyang Wu, and Changyu Jiao to lead some warriors to encircle Xi Qi, Xi Chou, and Xi Zhi and kill them with long dagger-axes. After that, Xu Tong kidnaped Luan Shu and Zhongxing Yan at the court and intented to kill them. But the duke stopped him and said, "Three officials have been killed, and I'm not willing to kill more. Free them, and let them resume their posts."

Luan Shu and Zhongxing Yan saved their lives through luck, but they thought a more permanent solution would be to kill the duke. One day, when the duke was drinking liquor and making merry with Lady Jiangli, Luan Shu and Zhongxing Yan suddenly arrested him and killed both Xu Tong and the duke. They then decided to support Zhou Zi, descendant of Duke Xiang, to be the new ruler. Zhou Zi was only fourteen years old at that time. When somebody suggested that his elder brother should be the successor to Duke Li, both Luan Shu and Zhongxing Yan replied, "Zhou Zi's elder brother cannot even tell beans from wheat, how can he be the sovereign of the state?" Zhou Zi was historically known as Duke Dao.

Zuo Qiuming's Chronicles

不學無術

bù xué wú shù

形容沒有學問，也沒有本事。

漢代大將軍霍光，功勛顯赫，掌握兵權長達四十多年，但他晚年時一子錯，滿盤皆落索。

漢宣帝劉詢即位時，立了許妃為皇后。霍光的妻子想把女兒嫁給劉詢做皇后，瞞著霍光，買通了女醫，趁許妃生病時下毒藥謀害了她。許妃死後，女醫被捕，關進大牢聽候審問。霍妻害怕事情敗露，才如實告訴了霍光，霍光想揭發妻子，又不忍她受罪，便包庇了妻子、女醫，把案情隱瞞了。霍光死後三年，案情終於暴露，劉詢派兵將霍氏家族、近親、遠親幾千戶人家搜捕、誅殺。

史學家班固評論霍光功過時說：“霍光敗於不學無術，不懂大道理，縱容包庇家人，才招致這樣悲慘的結局。”

出自《漢書》

不學無術

No Study, Know Nothing

Said of those lacking in both learning and practical ability.

Huo Guang, the Chief Marshal of the Han Dynasty, had performed outstanding feats for the court and was placed in command of the nation's armed forces for more than forty years. But in his later years, one careless move devalued his entire life.

When Liu Xun, known as Emperor Xuandi, ascended the throne,

Lady Xu was made Empress. Huo Guang's wife wanted her daughter to be the empress, so she managed to poison Empress Xu when she was ill, with the secret help of a female palace doctor, and she didn't let Huo Guang know anything about it. After the empress' death, the doctor was arrested and sent to jail to await trial. Afraid that the murder would be exposed, Huo Guang's wife finally told him the truth. Huo Guang wanted to denounce his wife, but he couldn't bear to see his wife tortured, so he harbored her and the doctor, and covered up the whole affair. Three years after Huo Guang's death the case was exposed, and Liu Xun had the Huo family and all their relatives arrested and killed.

Commenting on this incident, the famous historian Ban Gu said, "It was Huo Guang's failure to learn, his ignorance of common sense and, consequently, his connivance at his wife's evil-doing that resulted in such a miserable end."

History of the Han Dynasty

什襲珍藏

shí xí zhēn cáng

把物品一層層包裹收藏起來；形容十分珍重地把物品珍藏起來。

宋國有一個愚人，得到一塊燕石(形色像玉的石頭)，以為是罕有至寶。回家後，用上好的華櫃，丹黃色的緹巾一層又一層地包裹收藏著。周國有人知道了，要求宋人給他開開眼界。

周人看到石頭後，呵呵大笑起來："這是燕石，與瓦磚沒有分別。"宋人聽後，非常忿怒，把燕石更為珍藏起來。

出自《太平御覽》

Wrapping a Treasure Up Layer by Layer for Storage

Said of carefully treasuring something.

Once a fool in the Song State came by a Yanshan stone which looked very much like jade. He took it for a rare treasure and kept it in a fine box wrapped with layers of orange silk. One day someone from the Zhou State came and asked to look at it. But when he saw the stone, he couldn't help laughing and said, "It is a stone from Yanshan Mountain, and it's no dearer than a clay brick." The Song fool was angry at these words, and treasured the stone even more.

Taiping Imperial Encyclopedia

千變萬化

qiān biàn wàn huà

形容事物變化多端，無窮無盡。

西周時，周穆王在一次旅途中，遇見了多才多藝的偃師（魔術師）。他問偃師有甚麼新奇的本領。偃師便把假人拿出來，在他的操縱下，假人做出各種各樣的動作，還會唱歌跳舞。假人跳得很有節奏，動作優美，舞姿層出不窮。周穆王讚嘆説：“真是千變萬化，沒有窮盡呀！”

出自《列子》

One Thousand Changes and Ten Thousand Transformations

Said of the unending changes of things.

During the Western Zhou Dynasty, King Mu once met a versatile magician on one of his journeys. When asked what magic tricks he could do, the magician took out a puppet and made it sing and dance. The puppet danced rhythmically and gracefully, and the movements varied from time to time. The king gasped with admiration, "Its thousand and one changes are really fantastic!"

The Book of Lie Zi

千變萬化

升堂入室

shēng táng rù shì

登上廳堂，也進入內室；比喻學問由淺入深，到了很高的境界。

春秋時，子路是孔子的學生。有一天，孔子在廳堂裡與學生談話時，忽然問："子路為甚麼在這裡彈琴呢？"學生們回答不上，目光注視著子路以為孔子怪他無禮，在廳堂裡彈琴，表露出瞧不起的神色。孔子見到，連忙說："子路的學問已升堂，算不錯的了，但未入於室也。"

出自《論語》

Passing Through the Hall into the Inner Chamber

Said when someone reaches a high level in his studies and acquires profound scholarship.

In the Spring and Autumn Period, Zi Lu studied under the tutorship of Confucius. One day while giving a lecture to his disciples, Confucius asked suddenly, "Why is Zi Lu playing the zither here in the hall?" The disciples couldn't answer and glared at Zi Lu with spite, thinking that Confucius was criticizing his impoliteness for playing the zither in the hall. Noticing that, Confucius said hastily, "Zi Lu's learning is not bad; let us say, it has passed through the hall, but not entered into the inner chamber yet."

Confucian Analects

牛角掛書

niú jiǎo guà shū

牛角上掛著書；比喻勤奮好學。

隋末時的李密，雖家道中落，但他不以為恥，反而更勤奮讀書。有一天，李密騎牛外出，把書本掛在牛角上，邊上路邊讀了起來。宰相楊素坐著馬車從後而上，看到他在牛背上讀書，覺得奇怪，問道："你這學生，就哪麼用功啊？"李密回頭看見宰相，趕忙跳下牛背行禮，報了姓名。楊素與李密聊了一陣，覺得李密並非池中物。後來，李密成為起義軍的首領。

出自《新唐書》

Hanging a Book on an Ox Horn

Referring to people who are diligent and eager to learn.

Li Mi was born in the late years of the Sui Dynasty. At that time his family fortunes were at a low ebb, but he didn't think it shameful, and made up his mind to learn diligently. One day he rode out on an ox while attentively reading a book which was hanging on the ox horn. The Prime Minister Yang Su caught up with him from behind in his carriage and was surprised to see Li Mi reading a book while on an ox's back. He asked, "Hi, young man, why are you so diligent?" Turning round and seeing the Prime Minister, Li Mi jumped off the ox, made a salute, and gave his name. Yang Su talked with Li Mi for a while and found him to be anything but a mediocre person. As a matter of fact, Li Mi later became the leader of an insurrectionary army.

New History of the Tang Dynasty

文武之道，一張一弛

wén wǔ zhī dào, yī zhāng yī chí

比喻治理國家必須寬嚴相濟；也比喻工作和生活要善於勞逸結合。

有一次，孔子跟學生談論周文王、周武王治國之道說："治國的道理，有如拉弓箭一樣，把弓拉得太緊而不鬆弛一下，弓就會斷裂，文王、武王不會這樣做。弓鬆弛後不再拉緊，他們也不會幹的。一張一弛，就是文武治國之道了。"

出自《禮記》

The Principle of Kings Wen and Wu Was to Alternate Tension with Relaxation

Said of a leader who couples strictness with benevolence in running a state, or of people who know how to alternate work with rest.

Once Confucius talked with his disciples about the principle followed by kings Wen and Wu in governing the kingdom. He said, "The principle of administering a country is like drawing a bow. If a bow is drawn tightly all the way without slack, it will break. Kings Wen and Wu didn't follow that way. They also certainly didn't do things in such a way as to leave the bow always slack without ever being drawn tightly. Their principle was to alternate tension with relaxation."

The Book of Rites

以人為鑒

yǐ rén wéi jiàn

以別人作鏡子；比喻把人家的成敗得失為借鑒，使自已引以為戒。

魏徵是唐初傑出的政治家，他直言屢諫唐太宗。魏徵死後，唐太宗在朝廷嘆息說：“以銅為鏡，可以端正衣冠；以古為鑒，可以知道朝代興亡的原因；以人為鑒，可以辨明得失。我時常使用這三面鏡子，反省自已的過失。魏徵死了，我痛失一面鏡子啊！”

出自《舊唐書》

Using Others as Mirrors

Said of using the experiences of others for reference and reflection.

Wei Zheng was an extraordinary statesman of the early Tang Dynasty. He often spoke bluntly to Emperor Taizong. After his death, the emperor sighed at the court, "Using bronze as a mirror makes it easy to tidy ourselves up; using history as a mirror makes us clear about the cause of the rise and fall of dynasties; and using other people as a mirror makes us capable of weighing advantages and disadvantages. I often use the three mirrors to examine my faults. Now that Wei Zheng is dead, I have lost one mirror!"

Old History of the Tang Dynasty

以火救火，以水救水

yǐ huǒ jiù huǒ, yǐ shuǐ jiù shuǐ

用火來滅火，引水來治水；比喻不但未能制止，反而助長其勢。

有一次，孔子的學生顏回打算幫助衛國國君治理國家。臨走時，他請教孔子治理國家之道。孔子說："衛國國君是個殘暴荒淫、專聽讒言的人，他不會聽你的忠言，還會把你殺掉。如果你委屈順從他，反而更助長他的淫威，這是以火救火，以水救水，反而助長其勢。"顏回聽從孔子的勸導，打消了去衛國的念頭。

出自《莊子》

Fighting a Conflagration with Fire and Controling a Flood with Water

Said of the act of encouraging an evildoer rather than stopping him.

Once Yan Hui, a disciple of Confucius, planned to go to the Wei State to help the ruler administer his state. Before leaving, he asked Confucius for the principles of running a state. Confucius said, "The ruler of Wei is a cruel and dissolute person, and he often believes slanderous talk. When you go there, he will never listen to your sincere advice, and may even kill you. If you compel yourself to obey him, it will only add to his despotic power. You know, to fight a conflagration with fire and to control a flood with water will only lend force to it." Yan Hui accepted Confucius' advice and gave up the idea of going to the Wei State.

The Book of Zhuang Zi

以管窺天

yǐ guǎn kuī tiān

從小竹管裡觀看天空；比喻見識狹隘。

扁鵲是春秋時的著名醫生。有一天，他途經虢國，聽見宮內外哭聲震天，原來是虢國太子死了。扁鵲問宮中守門人，太子患何病而亡？守門人答：“晨早雞鳴，太子血氣不時，正不勝邪，暴病而死。”扁鵲說能救治太子，守門人不信，不讓他進宮。扁鵲仰天嘆氣說：“唉，你是以管窺天，見識淺薄。我不用切脈望診，聽你所言已知病之所在。不信？你試診太子是否耳鳴鼻張，兩股間尚存溫熱。”後來，國君請扁鵲救治太子，不到一個月，太子竟完全康復了。

出自《史記》

Looking at the Heavens Through a Tube

Alluding to those who take a narrow view of things.

Bian Que was a famous doctor of the Spring and Autumn Period. One day while traveling to the state of Guo, he heard a loud cry announcing the death of the crown prince. He asked the palace gatekeeper the cause of the death. The gatekeeper answered that it was in the early morning when a sudden attack of a serious illness made the crown prince's blood circulation difficult, and then stopped his heartbeat. Bian Que said that he could revive the crown prince. The gatekeeper didn't believe this at all, and wouldn't permit him to go into the palace. Bian Que looked up at the sky and sighed, "Oh, people looking at the heavens through a tube always have meager knowledge! Young man, from your words I have already discovered the cause of the crown prince's illness. Believe it or not—you may now go and confirm if the crown prince is breathing faintly with his ears ringing, and if the inner sides of his thighs are still warm." Later the ruler of Guo asked Bian Que to save the crown prince, and surprisingly the crown prince was fully recovered within one month.

Records of the Historian

以貌取人

yǐ mào qǔ rén

以外貌來選擇人；比喻以外貌的美醜為標準來選用人才。

孔子的學生宰予，能言善辯，口甜舌滑，討得老師的歡心。日子一久，他暴露出又懶又無德行，孔子很厭惡他，說他不可救藥。

子羽也是孔子的學生，他相貌奇醜，孔子不大喜歡他。但子羽品德、學問俱好，處事公正。後來，子羽在各諸侯國游學，弟子眾多，聲望很高。孔子知道後，很有感觸地說："我以言辭取人，看錯了宰予；以外貌取人，看錯了子羽。"

出自《史記》

Judging a Person Solely by His Appearance

Said of evaluating a person on the basis of his appearance.

Zai Yu, a disciple of Confucius, had a smooth and eloquent tongue, which helped him win the favor of Confucius. As time went by, his laziness and moral demerits were exposed. Confucius was then disgusted with him, and said that he was hopeless. Zi Yu was also one of Confucius' disciples. His extreme ugliness made Confucius dislike him. But Zi Yu was of good moral character and fine scholarship, and he often judged things fairly. Later, when he traveled to teach in the various states, many disciples gathered to follow him and gradually he gained a high reputation. Knowing this, Confucius said with deep feeling, "I've overestimated Zai Yu by his words, and underestimated Zi Yu by his appearance."

Records of the Historian

以貌取人

以酒解酲

yǐ jiǔ jiě chéng

以酒來解酒；比喻用有害的方法去救急。

西晉名士劉伶，一生縱酒放誕。有一天，他喝醉了酒，醒來非常口渴，便叫妻子拿酒給他解渴。妻子把酒倒在地上，並且把盛酒的器皿也打破了，痛哭流涕地勸道："你喝得太過分了，這是很傷身體的，你一定要戒掉酒癮。"劉伶說："很好，但我不能自制。唯有當著鬼神面前發誓戒酒。你趕快張羅酒肉，好讓我發誓吧。"

妻子把酒肉供奉神前，劉伶跪著祝誓道："天生劉伶，以酒為名，一飲一斛，五斗解酲，婦人之言，慎不可聽。"說完，便飲酒食肉，醉得不省人事。

出自《世說新語》

Drinking More to Cure Drunkenness

Said of meeting an urgent need with a harmful method.

Liu Ling, a scholar of the Western Jin Dynasty, indulged in drinking alcohol all his life. One day when he awoke from a drunken stupor he felt very thirsty and asked his wife to give him some alcohol to quench his thirst. His wife poured the alcohol on the ground, broke the drinking vessels, and said, "Your indulgence in drinking will badly hurt your health. You must give it up!" Liu Ling said, "You're right, but I often can't control myself. Only by vowing in the face of the god can I give up drinking. You'd better quickly prepare alcohol and meat for my rite of oath making."

When his wife placed the alcohol and meat on the sacrificial table,

Liu Ling knelt down and vowed, "Liu Ling as I am, loving alcohol is my fame; one *hu* goblet for each time, and five *dou* jars more can neutralize my drunken senses; be careful, women's words are always nonsense." Then he began to drink the alcohol and eat the meat until he was completely inebriated.

New Social Anecdotes

太歲頭上動土

tài suì tóu shàng dòng tǔ

在歲星方位破土動工；比喻不畏強權，觸犯權威。

古代天文學喻木星為歲星，歲星十二年一個循環，將黃道分為十二等份，歲星所在的部分為歲名。太歲自西向東運行，所經過的方位為凶方。迷信的傳說是在凶方禁忌動工，興建土木。

出自《論衡》

Breaking Ground Where the God of the Year Presides

Beard the Lion in His Den

Meaning defying the almighty.

The planet Jupiter was called Star of the Year in ancient Chinese astronomy. It takes twelve years for it to move one circle around the sun, and divides the ecliptic in twelve equal parts, each of which has its specific name. When Jupiter moves from west to east, its corresponding projected place on the earth will be an ill-omened place. According to the superstitious legend, one should avoid breaking ground at this inauspicious place.

Discourses Weighed in the Balance

四分五裂

sì fēn wǔ liè

整體分離四份，裂開五份；形容支離破碎，極為分散而不統一。

戰國時期，由於六國採用了蘇秦的合縱術，聯合起來對付秦國，使秦國不敢輕啟戰事。張儀是連橫術的主張者，他幫助秦國破解蘇秦六國聯盟的合縱術。張儀跑到魏國，對魏王說："魏國處於楚、韓、趙、齊四國之間，魏國無論與哪一國交惡，都會受到四國的進攻，與他們聯合，終會導致國家的四分五裂。六國合縱也只是暫時性的，不如與秦國結盟，免遭亡國。"魏王被說服了。

張儀用同樣的策略，利用各國的私心，實行各個擊破，終於瓦解了六國聯盟，蘇秦的合縱術也徹底失敗了。

出自《戰國策》

Break into Four Parts, and Each Part Cracks into Five Pieces

At Sixes and Sevens

Said of being in disorder, or rent by disunity.

During the Warring States Period, the Qin State dared not attack the other six states rashly because they had adopted Su Qin's Vertical Theory and united to resist Qin together. Zhang Yi was an advocate of the Horizontal Theory, and he planned to help Qin disrupt the alliance. He went to Wei first and said to the king, "Your state is with the four states: Chu, Han, Zhao, and Qi. Whichever state you fall out with, the four states are certain to attack you. To unite with them will result in the split of your state into many parts in the end. Besides, the alliance of the six states is only a temporary solution. It would be better to ally with Qin to avoid the fall of your own state." The king was convinced.

Taking advantage of the selfish consideration of each state, Zhang Yi used the same method to convince the rulers of the other states and the alliance finally disintegrated. Su Qin's Vertical Theory turned out to be a complete failure.

Anecdotes of the Warring States

四海之內皆兄弟

sì hǎi zhī nèi jiē xiōng dì

四海之內都有兄弟；比喻天下的人都像自己的兄弟一樣。

司馬牛和子夏都是孔子的弟子。有一天，司馬牛唉聲嘆氣地對子夏說："別人都手足情深，和睦相處，多羨慕人家呀！可我沒有兄弟，孤單一人過日子。"子夏安慰他說："不要難過嘛，君子只要謹慎不失，對人謙恭有禮，信守諾言，四海之內都有自已的好兄弟。何必為沒有親兄弟而介懷哩。"

出自《論語》

All Men Are Brothers Within the Four Seas

This is a way of saying all the people in the world are brothers.

Sima Niu and Zi Xia both were disciples of Confucius. One day Sima Niu complained sadly, "How I admire those people living amicably with their brothers! I'm unlucky to have no brothers and live all by myself." Zi Xia comforted him, "Don't be sad. If a gentleman always conducts himself in society carefully, treats others politely, and keeps his promises faithfully, all the people within the four seas will be his brothers. So why care about not having a blood brother so much?"

Confucian Analects

四海之內皆兄弟

目不見睫

mù bù jiàn jié

眼睛看不到自己的眼睫毛；比喻沒有自知之明。

楚國的楚莊王打算征伐越國，擴大自已的領土。楚莊王想乘越國國事混亂，社會百病叢生，兵馬軟弱之時，趁機打敗越國。杜子知道了這事後，來見楚莊王說："我雖然是個愚魯的人，但還知道人的智慧和眼睛一樣，往往能看清百步之外而看不見自已的睫毛。楚國不也是兵馬軟弱，國事混亂，盜匪橫行嗎？楚國比越國好不了多少，卻要去攻打人家，這太沒有自知之明了。"楚莊王聽了杜子的一席話後，取消了征伐越國的計劃。

出自《韓非子》

The Eye Cannot See Its Lashes

Said of people lacking in self-knowledge.

King Zhuang of the Chu State planned to attack Yue to enlarge his territory. At that time, the state affairs of Yue were in a mess with all kinds of corrupt practices prevailing, and its military forces were comparatively weak. The king of Chu wanted to take advantage of the present disorder in Yue and defeat it. Knowing the king's plan, Du Zi came to have an audience with the king. He said, "Though I'm a slow-witted man, I know that a person's wisdom is similar to his eyes which can clearly see things a hundred paces away, but not his own lashes. Don't you know the state of Chu is also in great disorder with misadministration of state affairs, weak military forces, and rampant banditry? Since the present situation of Chu is no better than Yue, in trying to attack Yue Chu will prove herself lacking in self-knowledge." Hearing Du Zi's words, the king gave up his plan.

The Book of Han Fei Zi

白雲親舍

bái yún qīn shě

白雲之下，父母居住之處；比喻人們遠離家鄉，常常思念父母。

狄仁傑是唐代的著名大臣，也是出名的孝子。有一次，他登上太行，看到天上的白雲往雙親居住的方向飛去，不禁心馳神往。良久，對左右隨從說："我的父母就是居住在白雲之下。"等到白雲飄蕩而去，才繼續上路。

出自《新唐書》

Parents Living Under the White Clouds

Said of wandering children remembering their parents.

Di Renjie was a famous court official in the Tang Dynasty, and also known as a devoted son. One day, when he stood at the top of Mount Taihang, and saw the white clouds in the sky drifting in the direction of his parents' home, his thoughts also flew with the clouds. After a while, he said to his attendants, "My parents are living under those patches of white clouds." He didn't move on until the clouds drifted far away.

New History of the Tang Dynasty

付諸洪喬

fù zhū hóng qiáo

付託於殷洪喬；比喻書信遺失。

晉朝時候，殷洪喬將要出任豫章太守。臨行時，京城的親朋戚友託他帶了百多封書信。當殷洪喬行到河邊時，把所有書信投入水中，說："沉者自沉，浮者自浮，殷洪喬不為致書郵。"

出自《世說新語》

Putting Letters in Hongqiao's Charge

To ask Yin Hongqiao to deliver the letters; said of letters that get lost.

In the Jin Dynasty there was a man called Yin Hongqiao who was to go to his new post as prefect of Yuzhang. Before he left, his relatives in the capital entrusted him with hundreds of letters and asked him to deliver them. But one day while at a river, he threw all the letters into the water and said, "It's none of my business whether you sink or float. Yin Hongqiao will never be a postman!"

New Social Anecdotes

立於不敗之地

lì yú bù bài zhī dì

處於不會失敗的位置上；任何情況都不會失敗。

孫武是春秋時期傑出的軍事家，他在所著的《孫子兵法》中說："善於作戰者，能發現對方的弱點，利用地利而取勝。善於防守者，利用山川地勢之險，使對方無處可攻；善於進攻者，利用天時地利，在對方沒有防備下，閃電攻擊。因此，善於作戰者要使自已立於不敗之地，還要掌握導致對方失敗的機會。"

出自《孫子》

Establishing Oneself in an Unassailable Position

Said of a person who occupies an impregnable position and is invincible.

Sun Wu was a great strategist in the Spring and Autumn Period. He wrote in his book *The Art of War* by Sun Zi: A person adept in conducting military operations always discovers the enemy's weak points and takes advantage of a favorable position to defeat the enemy; a person adept in defense always takes advantage of inaccessible and perilous terrain to make the enemy feel it is too difficult to attack; a person adept in attacking always takes advantage of a favorable opportunity and position to spring a surprise attack on the enemy. In a word, it's important for a good general to grasp a favorable opportunity to make himself invincible.

The Book of Sun Zi

出言不遜

chū yán bù xùn

說話無禮，態度傲慢。

三國時，袁紹和曹操在官渡兩軍對峙，準備進行決戰。當時，袁紹兵多糧足，自以為穩握勝券，疏忽了屯積糧草的烏巢遠離大本營，而且只派少量駐軍守衛。張郃發現了這個薄弱點，向袁紹建議：“派兵增援烏巢，防備曹軍搶奪糧草。”但郭圖反對，主張強兵攻打曹軍大營。袁紹同意郭圖的主張，派張郃領兵攻曹。結果，烏巢被曹軍攻破，糧草被燒光，攻曹營的戰事也失利。郭圖知道自已的主張錯了，在袁紹面前誣陷張郃在背後說他壞話，出言不遜，言辭傲慢。另方面，郭圖派人對張郃說袁紹要處死他。張郃懼怕，便率兵投降了曹操。

出自《三國志》

Making Impertinent Remarks

Said of someone speaking rudely and arrogantly.

In the Three Kingdoms Period, Yuan Shao and Cao Cao's troops confronted each other at a place called Guandu and were prepared for a decisive battle. At this time, Yuan Shao commanded a larger army with greater provisions and he took success for granted. But he neglected the fact that his granary at Wuchao was far away from the base camp, and was defended only by a small garrison. Zhang He found this weak point and advised Yuan Shao to send more troops to reinforce Wuchao and prevent Cao Cao's troops from making a sudden attack.

But Guo Tu disagreed with Zhang He and favored storming Cao Cao's camps with full strength. Yuan Shao followed this advice and ordered Zhang He to lead troops to attack Cao Cao's camps. Later, Wuchao was captured by Cao Cao's troops and the provisions were all set afire. Moreover, the attack on Cao's camps also turned out to be a failure. Realizing his serious error, Guo Tu told Yuan Shao that Zhang He had spoken ill of Yuan Shao and made impertinent remarks behind his back. At the same time, Guo Tu sent his henchman to tell Zhang He that Yuan Shao was going to kill him. Zhang He was frightened and surrendered his troops to Cao Cao.

History of the Three Kingdoms

平易近人

píng yì jìn rén

態度和靄可親，使人容易接近。

周公是西周時期的政治家，名字叫姬旦。因為采邑（受封的土地）在周，故稱為‘周公’。有一年，周公被封於曲阜為魯公，但他仍留在都城，派兒子伯禽受封，去曲阜為魯公。三年後，才報告當地政事給周公。周公說：“為甚麼這樣遲呢？”伯禽說：“改變風俗，革新禮法，非三年不可，所以來晚了。”封於齊地才五個月的姜尚這時也來報告政事給周公。周公說：“為甚麼這樣快呢？”姜尚說：“我簡化君臣之禮，從其為俗。”周公嘆氣說：“唉，魯的後世要敗於齊！政不簡、不平易，百姓不會歸順；為政平易近民的，百姓必會歸服。”

出自《史記》

平易近人

Amiable and Easy to Approach

As Comfortable As an Old Shoe

Said of a person who is easy to get along with.

Ji Dan was a statesman of the Western Zhou Dynasty. He was also called Duke Zhou for his feud was in the Zhou capital. One year he was appointed Duke Lu of Qufu, but he gave this post to his son Boqin instead of going there himself. Three years later, Boqin came and reported on local government affairs to Duke Zhou. Duke Zhou asked, "Why are you so late?" Boqin replied, "It was necessary to take three years to bring about a change in the morals and habits of the people. That's why I'm late." At this moment Jiang Shang, who had been enfeoffed in Qi for only five months, also came to report on the government's performance to Duke Zhou. Duke Zhou asked, "Why are you so early?" Jiang Shang replied, "I just simplified the proprieties between superiors and inferiors and had them follow the ordinary customs." Duke Zhou sighed, "Oh, Lu will be defeated by Qi in the future! If the administration is not simplified and benevolent, the common people will not pay allegiance to the government; but if it is amiable and easy to approach, it is sure to gain their allegiance."

Records of the Historian

汗牛充棟

hàn niú chōng dòng

比喻藏書極多。

陸淳是唐代的經學家，畢生致力研究《春秋》，留下著作甚多。文學家柳宗元說他的藏書放滿整個屋子，用牛馬運書，牛馬也累得出汗。

出自《陸文通先生墓表》

Enough Books to Make a Pack-Ox Sweat Or to Pile Ceiling-High

Used in reference to an immense collection of books.

Lu Chun, a specialist in Confucian classics during the Tang Dynasty, devoted himself to the study of the Spring and Autumn Annals all his life. He kept a great many works. The writer Liu Zongyuan said that the books Lu Chun collected filled the entire room and that a pack-ox or horse would sweat if it tried to carry them.

Epitaph for Lu Chun

汗流浹背

hàn liú jiā bèi

流出的汗水濕透脊背；形容極度恐懼或慚愧，也形容渾身淌汗。

漢文帝劉恆經常過問國事，有一次，他問右丞相周勃：“天下一年之中判決訴訟多少案件？”周勃説：“不知道。”漢文帝又問：“天下一年之中錢穀收支多少？”周勃又説不知道。周勃這時急得汗水濕透了脊背，又驚又愧答不出話來。

出自《史記》

Sweat Streaming Down and Drenching One's Back

Used to describe great fear or shame. Also used to describe profuse sweating.

Liu Heng, Emperor Wendi of the Han Dynasty, often attended to state affairs diligently. Once, he asked the Prime Minister of the Right, Zhou Bo, "How many sentences are passed in a year under heaven?" Zhou Bo replied, "I don't know." Then Emperor Wendi asked, "How much revenue and expenditures are there in a year under heaven?" Again, Zhou Bo said he had no idea. Zhou Bo was so frightened and ashamed that sweat drenched his back.

Records of the Historian

羊左之交

yáng zuǒ zhī jiāo

羊角哀與左伯桃是好朋友；比喻生死之交的朋友。

春秋時，羊角哀和左伯桃相約一同投靠楚國，不料半路上被大雪阻住。他們帶不夠衣食，如果一同前去楚國，兩人都會凍餓死去。左伯桃認為自己的才能不如羊角哀，就把自己的衣食留贈給他，催促他上路，自己就藏在樹穴裡死去。

羊角哀到了楚國後，顯名於世。有一天，羊角哀伐倒大樹，將左伯桃的屍體安葬好後，悲痛嗚咽："我的好友之所以死，是因為不想同死無益，卻沒有因此而名揚天下！如今我獨存下來，還有何用？"說完，也自殺而死。

出自《古今小說》

Friendship Between Yang Jiaoai and Zuo Botao

Used in reference to friends sworn to live or die together.

In the Spring and Autumn Period, Yang Jiaoai and Zuo Botao reached an agreement that they would go and seek refuge in the state of Chu. Unexpectedly, heavy snow blocked them halfway. Since they did not have enough food or clothing with them, they would freeze and starve to death if they both continued their journey to Chu together. Considering that Yang Jiaoai was more talented, Zuo Botao left his food and clothes with Yang Jiaoai and urged him to continue the journey. As a result, Zuo Botao died in the hollow of a tree.

After reaching the state of Chu, Yang Jiaoai became well-known throughout the state. One day, while cutting down the tree and burying the body of Zuo Botao, Yang Jiaoai sobbed with grief, "My good friend preferred to die alone rather than let me die uselessly together with him, but he didn't become famous for this all over the state. Now I have survived alone, but what's the use of that?" After these words, he committed suicide.

Stories Ancient and Modern

米珠薪桂

mǐ zhū xīn guì

米貴得如珍珠，柴禾貴得如桂木；形容物價昂貴。

蘇秦有一年來到楚國，他跟近侍說要拜見楚王。蘇秦以為楚王會立即接見他，誰知三天過後，楚王才召見他。蘇秦進宮後，與楚王寒喧了幾句便要告辭。楚王說："我仰慕你像仰慕先賢一樣，你不遠千里來到楚國，怎麼一刻也不肯停留？"蘇秦說："楚國的食糧比白玉貴，柴禾比桂樹貴，近侍難見得如見鬼，大王難見得如見天帝，難道要我食白玉、燒桂木，等鬼引見天帝嗎？"楚王明白了原因，便挽留蘇秦留在楚國。

出自《戰國策》

Rice as Precious as Pearls and Firewood as Costly as Cassia

Alluding to exorbitantly high prices.

One year, Su Qin came to the state of Chu and told a palace attendant that he would pay a formal visit to the king. Su Qin thought the king would receive him at once, but he had to wait for three days to see the king. After entering the palace, Su Qin exchanged a few words of greetings with the king and then he wanted to take his leave. The king said, "I admire you as much as I admire the sages of the past. You made light of travelling from afar before reaching the state of Chu. Why not stay a bit longer?" Su Qin said, "In the state of Chu, grain is more precious than pearls and firewood more expensive than cassia; palace attendants are as difficult to see as ghosts and Your Majesty as difficult to see as the Lord of Heaven. Will I eat pearls, burn cassia, and wait for a ghost to present me to the Lord of Heaven?" The king understood this, and urged Su Qin to stay in the state of Chu.

Anecdotes of the Warring States

安於故俗，溺於舊聞

ān yú gù sú, nì yú jiù wén

安於舊習俗，沉溺於舊見聞；形容安於現狀，因循守舊。

秦孝公六年，商鞅被任命為左庶長，開始實行變法。商鞅在制定新法令時，受到朝中一些守舊的大臣反對，商鞅和他們唇槍舌戰，駁斥他們説："平常人安於舊風俗，沉溺於舊的見聞。這兩者做官守法是可以的，但不能與他們論變法、革新之理。賢者、智者變法革新，愚者、保守者不明變通之道，才會阻攔變法。"秦孝公支持商鞅變法，使秦國逐漸成為強國。

出自《史記》

Satisfied with Old Customs and Outdated Information

Meaning satisfaction with the existing state of affairs and sticking to old ways.

In the sixth year of the reign of Duke Xiao of the Qin State, Shang Yang was appointed Grandee of the Tenth Order, and began to introduce institutional reform. By enacting new laws and decrees, Shang Yang was opposed by some conservative ministers at court. In a battle of words, Shang Yang refuted them, "Common people are satisfied with old customs and outdated information. We can let them act as officials and observe the laws, but we can't discuss institutional reform and innovation with them, as these are introduced by people of virtue and wisdom but resisted by foolish and conservative people because of their ignorance of the principle of adaptation." Duke Xiao supported Shang Yang's reform, which made the state of Qin strong step by step.

Records of the Historian

老嫗能解

lǎo yù néng jiě

老婆婆都能明白；比喻通俗易懂。

白居易是唐代的大詩人，他主張文章合為時而著，歌詩合為事而作。白居易的詩抨擊權貴，揭露時弊，同情民間疾苦。他的詩作題材廣泛，語言通俗。他作詩時，常讀給家中年老的僕婦聽，如果她們聽得明白，就記錄下來；如果不懂，就改寫至她們能解。

出自《冷齋夜話》

Intelligible to an Old Woman

Referring to something popular and easy to understand.

Bai Juyi, a great poet of the Tang Dynasty, maintained that some writings were famous for being in fashion, while poems were composed to confront social problems. His poems attacked influential officials, disclosed the ills of the times, and sympathized with the common people in their suffering. His poetical works had wide-ranging themes and used popular language. While composing, he often read to the old maid servants in his family. If they could understand him, he would be satisfied; otherwise, he would make revisions until they understood him.

Night Talks at Cool Studio

死不瞑目

sǐ bù míng mù

死了也閉不上眼睛；形容生前有未了之事，死後也不甘心。

東漢末期，董卓擁兵自重，廢漢少帝，立漢獻帝，殺了何太后，專斷朝政。孫策和袁術起兵討伐董卓。董卓懼怕孫策猛壯，派遣將軍李傕請求和親，孫策堅拒說：“董卓逆天無道，傾覆王室，不殺他全族，不把他懸首昭告天下，我死不瞑目！”

出自《三國志》

Dying Without Closing One's Eyes

Turn in One's Grave

Used to describe one's dissatisfaction after death because of leaving unfinished business behind.

At the end of the Eastern Han Dynasty, Dong Zhuo, counting on his great army to raise his status, dethroned Emperor Shaodi, designated Emperor Xiandi, killed Empress Dowager He, and acted arbitrarily at court. So, Sun Ce and Yuan Shu dispatched troops to suppress Dong Zhuo, who, fearing Sun Ce's valor and great strength, sent General Li Cui to ask for peace by marriage. Sun Ce firmly refused, "Dong Zhuo did godless things and subverted the imperial court. I will die without closing my eyes unless I kill his whole clan and cut off his head and display it in public."

History of the Three Kingdoms

死不瞑目

百折不撓

bǎi zhé bù náo

百次曲折也不會彎曲；形容無論受到多少次挫折，都不畏縮或屈服。

橋玄是東漢漢靈帝時的名臣，他剛正不阿，不畏權貴。他曾因兒子被強盜所擄，拒付贖款，寧可喪子也不姑息養奸。在朝中也曾遭受打擊報復，但他仍然檢舉大臣的罪行。有一次，他告發太中大夫蓋升搜刮民脂民膏的罪行，按律法應以治罪。可是皇帝與蓋升關係密切，不但不治蓋升的罪，反而讓他升官。橋玄一氣之下，辭官歸故里。

曹操那時是東漢的一個小官，常常和橋玄談論天下大事，兩人知交甚篤。後來曹操掌了大權，特意到橋玄墓前吊唁，並請中郎將蔡邕寫了一篇《太尉橋公碑》頌揚橋玄："其性莊，疾華尚樸，有百折不撓，臨大節而不可奪之風。"

出自《後漢書》

Never Bending in Spite of Repeated Twisting

Used to describe undaunted persistence in spite of repeated setbacks.

Qiao Xuan was a minister during the reign of Emperor Lingdi of the Eastern Han Dynasty, renowned for being upright, never stooping to flattery, and fearless before influential officials. Once his son was seized by robbers, but Qiao Xuan refused to pay ransom, preferring to lose his son rather than indulge kidnappers. At court, he once faced retaliation but he still accused some ministers of committing crimes. He charged Gai Sheng, Superior Grand Master of the Palace, with fleecing the people, and said he should be punished according to law. But the emperor, having close relations with Gai Sheng, promoted him instead of punishing him. In a fit of anger, Qiao Xuan resigned and returned home.

Cao Cao, then a petty official of the Eastern Han Dynasty, often talked with Qiao Xuan about major events under heaven. The two were devoted in friendship. When Qiao Xuan died, Cao Cao, who had mounted into prominence by now, specially expressed condolences before Qiao Xuan's tomb, and asked Cai Yong, Leader of the Court Gentlemen, to write on his tombstone: "Minister Qiao Xuan. Solemn by nature, he hated luxury and upheld simplicity. He never yielded in spite of repeated setbacks, nor gave in on issues of principle!"

History of the Later Han Dynasty

百折不挠

有志者事竟成

yǒu zhì zhě shì jìng chéng

有堅定意志的人最終會取得成功。

東漢初期，光武帝劉秀派遣耿弇征討割據勢力張步。耿弇很快就攻下臨淄、西安。張步氣惱萬分，親率二十萬大軍攻打耿弇。耿弇避其鋭氣，候至有利戰機，率精兵攻入張步軍中。這時，耿弇被流箭射中大腿，他咬牙抽刀截斷箭桿，繼續領軍殺退張步。戰情持續數日，有部將勸耿弇休戰等候援軍。耿弇不聽，連續作戰，把張步殺得慘敗而逃。劉秀稱讚説："耿弇的功績可以和韓信相比，連續奮戰，取得節節勝利，有志者事竟成呀！"

出自《後漢書》

A Man with a Set Purpose Will Finally Succeed

Where There's a Will There's a Way

Meaning nothing is impossible to a willing mind.

Early in the Eastern Han Dynasty, Liu Xiu, known as Emperor Guangwu, sent Geng Yan on a punitive expedition against the separatist regime of Zhang Bu. Soon, Geng Yan captured the cities of Linzi and Xi'an. In a fury, Zhang Bu himself led an army of two hundred thousand strong to attack Geng Yan, who, avoiding Zhang Bu and waiting for a favorable opportunity, led special troops in an assault. In this encounter, Geng Yan's leg was hit by a flying arrow. Clenching his teeth and drawing his sword to cut off the arrow shaft, he continued to lead his troops in beating back Zhang Bu. The battle lasted several days, and some officers tried to persuade Geng Yan to accept a truce and wait for relief troops. But Geng Yan wouldn't listen. He continued to fight, inflicting a crushing defeat on Zhang Bu, who fled away. Liu Xiu praised him, "Geng Yan can match Han Xin in merit and achievements, fighting hard successively and winning victory after victory. Well, really, as the saying goes, 'A man with a set purpose will finally succeed.' "

History of the Later Han Dynasty

有名無實

yǒu míng wú shí

徒有虛名而無實際。

春秋時，晉國太傅叔向在路上遇見韓宣子，韓宣子發牢騷地說："我有卿士之名而無財產之實，貧窮潦倒，比不上人家，為此憂心不已。"叔向開解他說："以前的晉大夫欒武子也是上卿，也並不富有，但他有德行，名望很高。郤昭子富可敵國，恃著權勢横行霸道，結果身受殺戮，宗族也滅亡了。我說呀，你應該憂心的是缺少德行，而不是缺少財富啊！"

出自《國語》

In Name but Not in Reality

Said of somebody or something that exists in name only.

In the Spring and Autumn Period, when Shu Xiang, Grand Mentor of the state of Jin, met Han Xuan Zi on a street, the latter complained, "I'm a nominal nobleman, having no property and living in dire poverty. I can't match others and I worry about this." Shu Xiang tried to comfort him, "Grand Master Luan Wu Zi of Jin was also an impoverished nobleman. He was not rich, but he had high moral purpose and a great reputation. Whereas Xi Zhao Zi, a man of enormous wealth, misused his power and influence and played the tyrant. As a result, he was killed and his clan exterminated. I say, what you should worry about is the lack of moral attainment rather than the lack of wealth."

Anecdotes of the States

行不得也哥哥

xíng bù dé yě gē gē

摹擬鷓鴣鳥的叫聲；表示行路的艱難。

鷓鴣是一種羽毛黑白相雜的鳥類，生活在灌木和疏樹的山地，喜歡吃昆蟲和植物的種籽。鷓鴣生性害怕霜露，所以早晚都很少出來活動，夜晚棲息時，以樹葉蔽身。有趣的是牠們鳴叫時，習慣對啼，叫個不休。人們都說牠們的鳴叫聲很像在說：“行不得也哥哥，行不得也哥哥。”

出自《本草綱目》

The Road Is Hard and We Can't Go On (Xing-Bu-De-Ye-Ge-Ge)

Imitated chirping of a partridge, used in reference to a difficult march.

Partridges are birds with black and white checkered feathers. They live in mountainous regions that are covered with bushes and sparse trees, and they like insects and seeds. Fearing frost by nature, they seldom move in the morning or the evening; and as night falls, they perch with leaves covering their bodies. It is of interest to note that they chirp to each other endlessly. It is said that they chirp as if to say, "*Xing bu de ye ge ge, xing bu de ye ge ge.*" ("The road is hard and we can't go on.")

Compendium of Materia Medica

全無心肝

quán wú xīn gán

比喻喪盡天良，不知羞恥；也指不懂人情世故。

南朝皇帝陳後主(叔寶)在位時，沉迷酒色，不理朝政。當隋兵南下時，他倚恃長江天險，毫不在意。後來隋兵攻進宮中時，他和寵妃張麗華、孔貴嬪躲在井裡避難。終於被俘擄至長安。隋文帝釋放了他，給他三品官的待遇。每逢朝廷宴會，隋文帝下令不准奏江南的音樂，以免引起他亡國之痛。

有一天，監守陳叔寶的人稟告給隋文帝說："陳叔寶每次聚會後，自言自語說：'我參加朝廷的宴會時，沒有相稱的職位，但願得到一個官號就好了！’”隋文帝聽罷，笑罵著說：“叔寶全無心肝。”

出自《南史》

Totally Heartless

Used when someone is without conscience or shame. Also said of one not knowing the ways of the world.

When he was on the throne, Chen Shubao, Emperor Houzhu of Chen in the Southern Dynasties Period, indulged in wine and women and paid no attention to state affairs. As the army of the Sui Dynasty advanced south, he remained indifferent, believing that the Yangtze River, a natural barrier, would protect him. When the army Sui finally stormed into the palace, he and his favorite concubines Zhang Lihua and Kong Guipin took refuge in a well, but he was captured and brought to Chang'an. Emperor Wendi of the Sui Dynasty released him and treated him as a third-rank official. At court banquets, Emperor Wendi ordered that the music from the south should not be played lest it should arouse Chen's grief for the loss of his state.

One day, the person responsible for Chen Shubao reported to Emperor Wendi, "Each time after a gathering, Chen Shubao would say to himself, 'I went to court banquets without a title befitting my status. How I wish I could gain an official title!'" Hearing this, Emperor Wendi cursed with a laugh, "Shubao is totally heartless."

History of the Southern Dynasties

羽毛未豐

yǔ máo wèi fēng

羽毛還沒有長滿；比喻力量還不夠強大，也指年紀輕，經歷少。

戰國時期，蘇秦有一天來到秦國，游說秦王採取他的戰略吞併六國。但秦王並不予以信任，客氣地說：“秦國目前的力量還不足以吞併六國，正如羽毛不豐者，不可以高飛。”蘇秦只好怏怏而退。

出自《戰國策》

羽毛未豐

The Feather Is Not Yet Fully Grown

Wet Behind the Ears

Used in reference to one not yet very powerful. Also said of one still young and inexperienced.

One day during the Warring States Period, Su Qin came to the state of Qin to persuade the king to adopt his strategy for annexing the six other states. The king, however, did not trust him, and said politely, "At present, the state of Qin is not powerful enough to annex the six states, just as fledgling birds cannot fly high." Sulking, Su Qin then had to withdraw.

Anecdotes of the Warring States

回天之力

huí tiān zhī lì

能將運行過去的天拉回來的力量；比喻能挽救危亡的力量。

貞觀四年，唐太宗李世民下詔重修洛陽宮乾陽殿。御史張玄素力諫唐太宗說："陛下應以秦始皇為鑒，他因逆天而行，傳至二世而亡。陛下曾經下令拆毀宮殿，現在反過來又要重修，天下百姓如何心服！如果陛下一意孤行，那就比隋煬帝還要錯啊！太上皇曾下詔：'宮室過分奢侈者焚之'，請陛下三思。"唐太宗聽進了諫言，下詔停修宮殿。大臣魏徵讚嘆說："張公論事，有回天之力，可謂仁人之言呀。"

出自《新唐書》

Power Capable of Drawing Back a Moving Heavenly Body

Used in reference to a force capable of saving a perilous situation.

In the fourth year of the Zhenguan Period, Emperor Taizong of the Tang Dynasty issued an edict to rebuild Qianyang Hall in Luoyang Palace. Censor Zhang Xuansu tried hard to convince Taizong, "Your Majesty should use Qin Shi Huang, the first emperor of the Qin Dynasty, as a mirror. He did godless things, and these caused the downfall of the Qin Dynasty in the second generation. Your Majesty ordered the demolition of the hall, but now plans to rebuild it. How can the common people be sincerely convinced? If Your Majesty insist on having your own way, that will be a worse mistake than Emperor Yangdi of the Sui Dynasty. Your father issued an imperial edict that the palace should be burned if it became excessively luxurious. Please think carefully, Your Majesty." Taizong believed these words and ordered that the hall not be rebuilt. Commenting on this, Minister Wei Zheng said, "Zhang's argument is really that of a public-spirited person, strong enough to turn back the heavenly body from moving ahead."

New History of the Tang Dynasty

同甘共苦

tóng gān gòng kǔ

同享樂，共患難；比喻有福同享，有難同當。

燕國被齊國打敗後，國力從此衰弱。燕昭王想復興國家，便去請教郭隗。郭隗說："大王應該選賢與能，禮賢下士，招攬天下的賢士為燕國效力。"燕昭王求才若渴的消息傳開了，一些有本事的人都聚集到燕國來，其中有著名的賢士樂毅、鄒衍、劇辛等人，他們都為燕昭王出謀獻策。燕昭王也身體力行，誰家有喪事，他就去吊唁；那家生了孩子，他就去祝賀，與百姓同甘共苦。經過了二十八年的艱苦經營，燕國富強了。燕昭王命樂毅領軍攻齊，把齊國打得大敗。

出自《戰國策》

Sharing Joy and Woe

Sink or Swim together

Said of people going through thick and thin together or sharing the rough and the smooth with others.

After defeat by the state of Qi, the state of Yan remained weak from then on. King Zhao of Yan wanted to rejuvenate his kingdom, so he asked Guo Wei for advice. Guo Wei said, "Your Majesty should summon the able under heaven to serve the state of Yan, and treat them with courtesy." The news that King Zhao eagerly sought after men of worth and ability spread, and the state of Yan was able to gather some men of ability, including such famous men of worth as Yue Yi, Zhou Yan, and Ju Xin, who gave counsel to King Zhao. And King Zhao put into practice what he advocated. He expressed his condolences at funerals and offered his congratulations to families with newborn babies, sharing the joys and sorrows of the common people. After twenty-eight years of arduous efforts, the state of Yan became strong and prosperous. King Zhao ordered Yue Yi to lead troops to attack the state of Qi, which then suffered a crushing defeat.

Anecdotes of the Warring States

先下手為強

xiān xià shǒu wéi qiáng

先動手為強者；形容首先下手，可以取得優勢。

南北朝時，北周丞相楊堅很器重大將軍元冑。有一次，趙王招宴請楊堅，元冑懷疑趙王招在酒宴上設計謀害他，便陪同一起赴宴。在酒宴中，趙王招使出花樣支開元冑，好下毒手，可是元冑不為所動。後來，元冑乘趙王招不覺，耳語楊堅說：“趙王招想謀害你，趕快離開。”楊堅有些猶豫說：“他沒有兵馬，能有甚麼作為？”元冑急著說：“被他一先下手，大事便去矣，到時後悔莫及！”楊堅聽元冑勸告，藉機脫身回到相府。

出自《北史》

先下手為強

He Who Strikes First Prevails

The Early Bird Cathes the Worm

Referring to taking the initiative to gain the upper hand.

During the Southern and Northern Dynasties, Yang Jian, Prime Minister of the Northern Zhou Dynasty, thought highly of Chief Marshal Yuan Zhou. Once, when Yang Jian was invited to attend a banquet by Zhao Wangzhao, Yuan Zhou suspected a murder plot and attended the banquet with him. At this banquet, Zhao Wangzhao tried to find some pretext to make Yuan Zhou leave the room so as to lay his murderous hands on Yang Jian. Yuan Zhou, however, remained unmoved. Later, while Zhao Wangzhao was distracted, Yuan Zhou whispered in Yang Jian's ear, "Be off quickly, for Zhao Wangzhao wants to murder you." Yang Jian said hesitantly, "What can he do without any troops?" Yuan Zhou replied anxiously, "Once he strikes first, it's all over for you. Then it will be too late for regret." Yang Jian followed his advice and seized the chance to get away back to his residence.

History of the Northern Dynasties

先入為主

xiān rù wéi zhǔ

以先聽到的、先看到的為依據；比喻對事物的看法先有了偏見或成見。

漢朝時，漢哀帝寵信董賢、孫寵、息夫躬三人。但三人勾心鬥角，其中以董賢的權勢最大，息夫躬老想取而代之。有一次，息夫躬阻止單于來朝拜，然後哄騙皇帝説："匈奴單于以患病為由，今年不來朝拜，事有蹺蹊，説不定單于起兵侵犯邊境，請陛下派兵出征。"大臣們勸諫皇帝不要輕信息夫躬的話。丞相王嘉也勸説："天子應行德政，子民才可安居樂業。請陛下借鑒古戒，反覆參考，不能以先入之語為主。"漢哀帝不聽群臣的勸諫，還是命軍隊準備出征。

出自《漢書》

First Impressions Are Strongest

Referring to approaching problems according to what one first hears or sees.

During the Han Dynasty, Emperor Aidi favored and trusted Dong Xian, Sun Chong, and Xi Fugong, who meanwhile were conspiring against each other. Xi Fugong tried hard to replace Dong Xian, who enjoyed the greatest influence of the three. On one occasion, Xi Fugong prevented the chief of the Xiongnu tribe from paying obeisance to the emperor, whom he then told, "The Xiongnu chief didn't come to pay obeisance this year under the pretext of illness, so there's something fishy about it. Perhaps he will send troops to invade the border. Please dispatch troops on an expedition, Your Majesty." The ministers advised the emperor not to readily believe him. Prime Minister Wang Jia also advised the emperor, "The common people can live and work in peace and contentment only if Your Majesty pursues a benevolent rule. Please always use the ancient commandments for reference, and don't rely mainly on quick impressions." But Emperor Aidi turned a deaf ear to the ministers' advice, and ordered the troops to prepare for the expedition.

History of the Han Dynasty

先憂後樂

xiān yōu hòu lè

先擔憂後享樂；形容先承擔憂患，最後才享樂。

范仲淹是北宋時著名的政治家、文學家。他擔任參知政事時，向仁宗皇帝建議改革官制，重視農業，整頓武備，減輕徭役等。後被讒言所害，受到降職處分。有一年，他遊覽岳陽樓，有感而發，寫了《岳陽樓記》，抒發了體恤民間疾苦，憂國憂民的感情。文中的‘先天下之憂而憂，後天下之樂而樂’成為了千古名言。

出自《岳陽樓記》

Be the First to Show Concern and the Last to Enjoy Oneself

Used to describe one who, at every turn, thinks of others before himself.

Fan Zhongyan was a famous statesman and writer during the Northern Song Dynasty. In the capacity of Imperial Consultant he once suggested that Emperor Renzong reform the civil service system, give importance to agriculture, consolidate the armed forces, and reduce conscripted labor. He was later persecuted by slanderous talk, and demoted. One year, while visiting Yueyang Tower, he exploded with his ideas, writing Travel Notes on Yueyang Tower, in which he expressed the fervor of his solicitude for the sufferings of the common people and concern for his country. His phrase, "Be concerned before everyone else, and enjoy yourself only after everyone else finds enjoyment," became famous for all time.

Travel Notes on Yueyang Tower

先聲後實

xiān shēng hòu shí

先樹聲威而後繼以實力；比喻先以聲威震懾對方，而繼之以實力取勝。

楚漢相爭時，韓信打敗了趙王歇後，繼而想攻打燕國和齊國，他問計於廣武君。廣武君說："漢軍剛打過趙國，如果馬上攻打燕、齊，疲兵再戰，討不了便宜，同時也削弱了和楚項羽爭天下的實力。不如暫時休養生息，按兵不動，先安撫趙國，再游說燕、齊歸順，漢就可以得天下了。正如兵家常說的：'以聲勢懾服敵人為上策，用武力攻戰為下策。'"韓信言聽計從，果然取得了勝利。

出自《史記》

Proclaiming One's Might First and Then Demonstrating It

Referring to frightening the other party with a great display of strength first before winning a victory by actual strength.

After defeating the state of Zhao, General Han Xin of the state of Han planned to attack the states of Yan and Qi. When he asked Lord Guangwu of the state of Zhao for tactics, he was told, "You just attacked the state of Zhao. If your troops attack the states of Yan and Qi at once in a state of exhaustion, you will not gain advantage but weaken your strength in fighting for supremacy over Xiang Yu of Chu. For the moment, you'd better rest and build up your strength, keep the troops ready for battle, and pacify the state of Zhao before trying to persuade the states of Yan and Qi to come over to you. In this way the state of Han can achieve supremacy. As the saying of military strategists goes: 'Cowing the enemy into submission by making a big show of your strength is the best way, while attacking with military force is an unwise move.'" Acting upon Guangwu's advice, Han Xin achieved his victory.

Records of the Historian

先禮後兵

xiān lǐ hòu bīng

先以禮相待，後用武力解決；比喻先談判解決爭端，後用強硬手段解決。

三國時，曹操派兵圍困徐州，太守陶謙請求劉備率兵救援。劉備寫了一封信給曹操，勸曹操退兵。曹操看信後大怒，命人先斬來使，調動兵馬全力攻城。謀臣郭嘉勸諫說："劉備遠來救援徐州，採取先禮後兵，主公應好言安撫，鬆懈他們戒備之心，然後進兵攻城，城可破了。"曹操聽從了郭嘉的意見，善待使者，回信給劉備。

出自《三國演義》

Courteous Before Resorting to Force

Referring to settling disputes by negotiations before taking stronger measures.

During the Three Kingdoms Period, Cao Cao sent troops to besiege Xuzhou. Prefect Tao Qian then asked Liu Bei for relief troops. Liu Bei wrote a letter to Cao Cao, advising him to retreat. Furious after reading the letter, Cao Cao ordered that the envoy be executed and that his troops be moved for an all-out attack on the city. Counselor Guo Jia offered his advice, "Coming to the rescue of Xuzhou from afar, Liu Bei wants to treat us with courtesy first before resorting to force. Your Majesty had better pacify his troops with tactful words so as to relax their vigilance. Then we can send troops to capture the city." Cao Cao followed his advice, treating the envoy well and replying to Liu Bei.

Tales of the Three Kingdoms

先禮後兵

各得其所

gè dé qí suǒ

各自如其所願，每個人都得到所希望或需要的東西。

昭平君是漢武帝的女婿，倚仗皇親國戚的關係，橫行無忌。有一次，昭平君酒後殺人，論罪應判死刑。漢武帝很為難，妹妹隆慮公主臨死時請求他照顧昭平君。最後漢武帝不想壞了法制，處死了昭平君。漢武帝為此悶悶不樂，東方朔勸解他說："陛下已做到賞功不分仇敵，罰罪不論親疏，四海之內的平民百姓，各得其所。"

出自《漢書》

Each in His Own Place

Said when everyone gets justice.

Lord Zhaoping, the son-in-law of Emperor Wudi of the Han Dynasty, ran amuck relying on his kinship with the Emperor. Once, Lord Zhaoping committed murder after drinking, and should be sentenced to death according to law. Emperor Wudi was embarrassed, for his sister Princess Longlu, on her deathbed, had begged him to give Zhaoping preferential treatment. At last, unwilling to violate the legal system, Emperor Wudi executed Zhaoping, but was in low spirits afterward. So Dongfang Shuo comforted him, "Your Majesty gave rewards for merits and punishments for crimes, irrespective of enemies and relatives, so the common people throughout the whole nation can enjoy their own places."

History of the Han Dynasty

自慚形穢

zì cán xíng huì

自愧於形貌醜陋；形容自己不如人而感到慚愧。

衛玠是晉代時的名人，生於世宦之家，祖上都是做官。他一生下來就相貌非凡，儀態、風度都與別的孩子不同，人人見了都讚美不絕。驃騎將軍王濟是衛玠的舅舅，生得手俊健朗，風姿綽綽。有一天，他見到衛玠，感嘆地說：“衛玠和我相比，他像珠玉般晶瑩純潔，使我自覺形穢。”

出自《世說新語》

Ashamed of One's Ungainly Appearance

Used to describe one's shame at his or her inferiority.

Wei Jie, a man famous during the Jin Dynasty, was born of a family holding high official positions for generations. Since he was of extraordinary appearance by nature and carried himself in a way different from other children, people praised him again and again. General Wang Ji, Wei Jie's uncle, was himself handsome, frank, and graceful. One day, seeing Wei Jie, he sighed, "Compared with me, Wei Jie is glittering and pure like pearls and jade. This makes me ashamed of myself."

New Social Anecdotes

好整以暇

hào zhěng yǐ xiá

形容辦事既嚴整而又從容不迫。

春秋時，晉國攻打鄭國。楚國為救援鄭國，派子反、子重、子辛率軍迎戰晉國。雙方交戰下，不分勝負。晉國的欒鍼看到楚軍子重的旗幟，知道子重必在陣中，高聲説："子重，我到楚國的時候，你曾問我晉軍之勇何在？我説：'好以眾整，好以暇'。今兩國交鋒，不派使者，不可謂嚴整；臨事而食言，不可謂從容。你壞了規矩，現在我先派使者向你獻酒。"子重接過使者的酒一飲而盡後，説："好吧，現在我就擊鼓叫陣！"雙方又再度交戰了。

出自《左傳》

Remaining Composed in Difficult Situations

As Cool As a Cucumber

Said of remaining calm under pressure.

In the Spring and Autumn Period, the state of Jin attacked the state of Zheng. The state of Chu allowed Zi Fan, Zi Zhong and Zi Xin to help the state of Zheng. The two sides were fighting to a stalemate, but when Luan Zhen of Jin saw the flag of Zi Zhong he realized that Zi Zhong must be among the troops, and he shouted, "Zi Zhong, when I went to Chu, you asked me if the Jin troops were brave. I said remain composed when handling difficult situations. Today, as two states engage in battle, you did not send an emissary, that is not being composed; eating your words is not remaining calm. You broke that rule, and now, I will let my emissary offer you wine." Zi Zhong drank the wine at once, and said, "Well, I'll begin to attack by beating drums!" Two sides then went into battle again.

Zuo Qiuming's Chronicles

如出一口

rú chū yī kǒu

好像同一張嘴巴說出來；形容異口同聲，說法一樣。

燕國有一個人的妻子與一讀書人私通，燕人早出晚歸，毫不知情。有一天，燕人突然提早回家，讀書人剛巧幽會完出來。燕人問妻子："哪裡來的客人？"妻子回答說："沒有客人。"燕人問左右他人，左右人眾口同聲說："沒有客人。"

出自《韓非子》

Uttered As If from One Mouth

Speaking with One Voice

Said of unanimity of opinions.

A man of the state of Yan did not know that his wife was committing adultery with an intellectual, because he always went out early and came back late. One day, the man came back early just as the wife's lover left. The man asked his wife, "Where was that guest from?" His wife replied, "No guest." When the man asked others, they answered with one voice, "No guest."

The Book of Han Fei Zi

朽木糞牆

xiǔ mù fèn qiáng

腐爛的木頭和髒土臭泥砌的牆；比喻不堪造就的人或不可收拾的局面。

宰予是孔子的學生，他的模樣生得很好看，孔子原先很喜歡他。後來，孔子發覺他的德行不好，減少了對他的好感。有一天的白晝，孔子看見宰予在酣然大睡，就不滿地說：“朽木不可雕鏤，糞土之牆不可粉刷，這於宰予來說有甚麼分別！”

出自《論語》

Decayed Wood and Dirt Wall

You Can't Make a Silk Purse Out of a Sow's Ear

Said of a worthless fellow or a hopeless situation.

Zai Yu, a pupil of Confucius, was a good-looking man. Confucius liked him at first. Later on, Confucius found that he had bad moral integrity and this decreased his good opinion of him. One day, Confucius found Zai Yu sound asleep in the daytime, and he said with dissatisfaction, "Decayed wood can not be carved, a dirt wall can not be painted, and there is no difference between these things and Zai Yu!"

Confucian Analects

沆瀣一氣

hàng xiè yī qì

崔沆、崔瀣連成一氣；比喻氣味相投，互相勾結。

唐僖宗年間，有一讀書人崔瀣參加科舉考試，主考官崔沆取錄了他。原來崔瀣是崔沆的學生，當時人們譏笑他們："座主門生，沆瀣一氣。"後來形容氣味相投的人互相勾結。

出自《南部新書》

Hang and Xie Breathe the Same Breath

Cheek by Jowl

Said of people of the same ilk, or people acting hand in glove with each other.

During the time of Emperor Xizong of the Tang Dynasty, an intellectual named Cui Xie took part in the civil examination. The chief examiner, Cui Hang, enrolled him, because Cui Xie was his pupil. People at that time teased them, "Hang the teacher and Xie the pupil breathe the same breath."

New Book of the South

沐猴而冠

mù hóu ér guàn

獼猴戴上帽子；比喻虛有其表或地位，而無真本領。

楚霸王項羽，心裡懷念故鄉，想著回江東眩耀威風，但又走不開，很不甘心地說："得到了富貴而不回故鄉，就像黑夜裡穿著錦衣行走，哪有人知道呢？"

後來，有人說："人們都說楚國人沒有真本領，好像獼猴戴帽做個樣子罷了，果然如此！"

出自《史記》

A Monkey Wearing a Hat

Said of a worthless person in imposing attire.

Xiang Yu, known as the All-Conquering King, missed his hometown and wanted to visit it to flaunt his success. But being too busy to leave, he said unwillingly, "People who have attained wealth and honor but can't go back home seem to walk in the dark in embroidered dress—nobody will know him!"

Later, some said, "People always say that those from the state of Chu have no real talent, just like a monkey with a hat on. Indeed, there's something in what they say!"

Records of the Historian

言不由衷

yán bù yóu zhōng

說話不是發自內心；形容虛偽敷衍，言行不一。

春秋時期，鄭國的鄭莊公掌握了周朝的大權，周平王不得不由他處理朝政。周平王其實是相信忌父，想他取代鄭莊公。鄭莊公知道後，質問周平王，周平王加以否認。為了安撫鄭莊公，周平王與他交換兒子作為人質。周平王死後，孫子周桓王繼位。他也想忌父替代鄭莊公，鄭莊公大怒，派兵馬搶掠周朝的農作物。從此，周朝與鄭國結下了仇恨。

後來人們評論說："說話不發自衷心，即使交換人質也無益。如果互相信任，雖無人質，誰又能離間得了呢？"

出自《左傳》

The Words Spoken Are Not from the Heart

Speak with One's Tongue in One's Cheek

Meaning not to say what one thinks in one's mind.

In the Spring and Autumn Period, Duke Zhuang of the state of Zheng held the power of the Zhou Dynasty, and King Ping of Zhou had to let him deal with court affairs. But in fact, the king wanted Ji Fu to take the place of Duke Zhuang. Duke Zhuang questioned the king about this, but the king denied it. In order to appease Duke Zhuang, the king and the duke exchanged their sons as hostages. After the king died, his grandson King Huan ascended the throne. He also wanted Ji Fu to take the place of Duke Zhuang. Knowing this, Duke Zhuang raged and ordered his troops to sack the Zhou Dynasty granaries. After that, the Zhou Dynasty and the state of Zheng became enemies.

Later, people commented on it, saying, "It's useless to exchange hostages when talking insincerely. If both sides trust each other, their relations will be good even without hostage."

Zuo Qiuming's Chronicles

初出茅廬

chū chū máo lú

開始走出草屋；比喻剛涉足社會，缺乏經驗；也比喻剛出來工作。

三國時，劉備三請諸葛亮當軍師。關羽、趙雲、張飛等人不服氣，看不起諸葛亮。有一次，曹操派夏侯惇領軍攻打劉備，張飛故意為難諸葛亮，提議他去對付夏侯惇，劉備就讓諸葛亮調兵遣將。諸葛亮定下誘敵之計，放曹軍進入博望坡，埋下伏兵用火攻。果然夏侯惇中計，被殺得大敗而逃。後人讚揚諸葛亮說："博望相持用火攻，指揮如意笑談中。直須驚破曹公膽，初出茅廬第一功！"

出自《三國演義》

Just Coming out of the Thatched Cottage

A Greenhorn

Said of one completely inexperienced, or one at the beginning of his career.

During the Three Kingdoms Period, Liu Bei went three times to Zhuge Liang's country cottage to ask him to be his advisor. Not thinking much of Zhuge Liang, generals Guan Yu, Zhao Yun, and Zhang Fei were not convinced this was a good idea. When Cao Cao ordered Xiahou Dun to attack Liu Bei, Zhang Fei deliberately made things difficult for Zhuge Liang by suggesting that he deal with Xiahou Dun. Then Liu Bei placed Zhuge Liang in command of the forces. Zhuge Liang made a plan to lure Cao's troops into entering Bowang Hill and attack them with fire, putting Xiahou Dun's forces to rout. This poem commemorates Zhuge Liang, "*With fire he broke the battle at Bowang, All smiles and small talk, giving each his cue. Striking fear deep into Cao Cao's soul, Thus Zhuge Liang scored a coup at his debut.*"

Tales of the Three Kingdoms

初出茅廬

求仁得仁

qiú rén dé rén

求仁德就得到了仁德；比喻如願以償、得償所欲。

有一次，子貢問孔子說："叔夷、伯齊是怎麼樣的人？"孔子回答說："他們是古時候的聖賢。"子貢又說："他們有埋怨不滿嗎？"孔子說："他們互相禮讓君位，求仁而得仁，達到了仁德的境界，又怎會有怨呢？"

出自《論語》

Seeking Benevolence and Acquiring It

Said of obtaining a desired object.

Once Zi Gong asked Confucius, "What kind of people are Shu Yi and Bo Qi?" Confucius replied, "They were ancient sages." Zi Gong asked again, "Were they dissatisfied with something?" Confucius answered, "They willingly yielded the throne to each other, sought benevolence and acquired it, and attained virtue, how could they complain?"

Confucian Analects

赤膊上陣

chì bó shàng zhèn

光著上身上陣作戰；比喻剽悍、不顧一切的作風；也指脫下偽裝，毫不掩飾地從事。

東漢末年，馬超為父報仇，和韓遂聯手，前後攻擊曹軍。曹操抵擋不住，棄寨而逃。第二天，兩陣對壘，馬超提槍縱馬與曹操的悍將許褚大戰。兩人殺得難分難解，不分勝負。許褚殺得性起，奔回陣中，卸下盔甲，赤體提刀上馬，來與馬超決戰。兩軍見許褚如此剽悍，大為震駭。馬超也不示弱，兩人又惡戰連場。

出自《三國演義》

赤膊上陣

Going into Battle Stripped to the Waist

Said of throwing off all disguises.

In the late years of the Eastern Han Dynasty, in order to avenge his father Ma Chao united with Han Sui to pincer-attack Cao Cao's troops. Cao Cao couldn't hold his ground and had to escape. Next day, the two armies were pitted against each other. Ma Chao took a spear, and riding his horse went to attack Cao Cao's brave general Xu Chu. The two were then locked in battle, and at the crucial moment Xu Chu rushed to his position to take off his helmet and armor and came back stripped to the waist. Xu Chu was so brave and agile that the two armies were shocked. Ma Chao showed no weakness, as they fought fiercely again and again.

Tales of the Three Kingdoms

攻心為上

gōng xīn wéi shàng

從思想、心理狀態上瓦解對手的鬥志是最為高明的策略。

諸葛亮出師南征時，蜀國參軍馬謖向他獻計："南方偏遠，地勢險要，雖能以武力壓服，過後又會反叛。我的見解是：'用兵之道，攻心為上策，攻城為下策；心戰為上策，兵戰為下策。'"諸葛亮採用了馬謖的策略，使南方的孟獲心服口服，多年都沒有反叛。

出自《三國志》

Attacking the Enemy's Mind Is the Most Important of All

Meaning psychological offensive is the best tactic.

Before Zhuge Liang started his southern expedition, Councilor Ma Su suggested, "The southern tribesmen live in a place of remoteness and inaccessibility. Even if you conquer them today, they will rebel tomorrow. In my view, the enemy's mind is more important than his city: psychological struggle is superior to armed struggle." Zhuge Liang took Ma Su's advice and made the southern tribal chief Meng Huo admit the Shu Kingdom's superiority, and he did not rebel again for quite a long time.

History of the Three Kingdoms

吾道東矣

wú dào dōng yǐ

我的學説傳播到東方去了；表示自已的學術主張得到傳佈、推廣。

東漢鄭玄是著名的經學家、教育家。他曾拜在馬融門下學習古文經。但三年都未得到馬融的親自傳授，只是由馬融的得意弟子代師傳藝。鄭玄日夜攻讀，從不怠倦。

有一天，馬融召集門下弟子，考論他們的學業，因此知道鄭玄善於《易經》，於是便單獨召見他。鄭玄不放過這次難得的機會，提出許多疑難的問題。鄭玄疑難盡釋後，拜辭馬融回去了。馬融很有感觸地對弟子們說："鄭玄走了，吾道東矣！"

出自《後漢書》

My Theory Has Been Transmitted to the East

Said of spreading of one's ideas.

Zheng Xuan of the Eastern Han Dynasty was a famous Confucianist and educator. He didn't learn ancient classics from Ma Rong himself, but rather from Ma Rong's best pupil. Zheng Xuan studied diligently night and day.

One day, Ma Rong examined his pupils and discovered that Zheng Xuan was good at *The Theory of Change*. He then had a talk alone with Zheng Xuan. To sieze this opportunity, Zheng Xuan put forward many questions. After making all his questions clear, Zheng Xuan said farewell to Ma Rong. Ma Rong later told his pupils, "Zheng Xuan has left, and my theory will be transmitted to the East!"

History of the Later Han Dynasty

見利忘義

jiàn lì wàng yì

有利可圖就不顧道義；形容遇到有利益時，出賣朋友或罔顧公義。

漢高祖劉邦死後，呂后掌權。呂后為了安坐天下，便大權獨攬，並封侄兒呂產、呂祿為王，控制了軍政大權。可是呂后不得人心，遭到眾老臣將領的反對。以周勃、陳平為首的老臣密謀誅滅呂氏家族。周勃利誘呂祿的好朋友酈寄，終於誅殺了呂氏家族。酈寄因出賣呂祿有功，被封為將軍。

史學家班固記載這件事時說：“酈寄是出賣朋友的人，是見利而忘義了。”

出自《漢書》

Disregarding Moral Principles in Pursuit of Profit

Said of forgetting friendship or public good for the sake of profit.

After Emperor Gaozu (Liu Bang) of the Han Dynasty died, his wife, Dowager Lu, took power. In order to stabilize the country, Dowager Lu appointed her nephews Lu Chan and Lu Lu as princes to command military forces. But Dowager Lu was unpopular, and all the old officials and generals were against her. Led by Zhou Bo and Chen Ping, the old officials hatched a plan to destroy the Lu clan. By involving Lu Lu's good friend Li Ji in the plot, they at last killed all the members of the Lu clan. Li Ji was appointed as general for his betrayal of Lu Lu.

Historian Ban Gu recorded this event with this comment, "Li Ji betrayed his friend, so he forgot friendship for the sake of profit."

History of the Han Dynasty

見利忘義

防民之口，甚於防川

fáng mín zhī kǒu, shèn yú fáng chuān

堵塞民眾的嘴，比堵塞泛濫的川河還要難；比喻壓制言論的危害性。

西周的周厲王專橫殘暴，老百姓恨之入骨，到處罵他的暴行。卿士邵公勸告周厲王："你的作為，百姓已受不了啦，到處都在講你的暴行了。"周厲王不但不聽勸告，反而派人監視百姓，發現誰有不滿言論，就殺了誰。一時，老百姓敢怒而不敢言，仇恨的怒火只能埋在心裡。周厲王得意地對邵公說："現在還有誰敢講我的壞話嗎？"邵公嘆氣說："防民之口，甚於防川。堵塞了川河，河水泛濫成災，必成大禍，民亦如是。所以，治理川河須要疏導，治理百姓，要允許他們宣洩不滿，這樣天下才可安定。"

周厲王不理邵公的忠言，一意孤行。三年之後，終於激起民憤，暴動四起，把周厲王趕跑了。

出自《國語》

Stopping People's Mouths Is More Difficult Than Damming Rivers

Said of the danger that may result from attempts to stifle freedom of speech.

King Li of the Western Zhou Dynasty was authoritative and cruel, so people hated him to their bones and cursed his savage acts everywhere. Minister Shaogong advised King Li, "People can't bear your behavior, so they talk about your savage acts everywhere." Instead of taking his advice, the king appointed his henchmen to keep watch on the people. Whoever was found to have any complaint would be killed. Now, people were furious, but they didn't dare to say anything. They had to bury the flames of anger in their hearts. The king said to Shaogong with pleasure, "Now, who dares speak ill of me?" Shaogong sighed, "To stop people's mouths is more difficult than blocking up rivers. If rivers are blocked up, it will cause disastrous floods, so with people. To control rivers you need to dredge; to control people, you must permit them to express their dissatisfaction. Only in this way can society be stable."

But the king acted in disregard of Shaogong's advice. Three years later, the people rebelled, and the king was forced to flee.

Anecdotes of the States

吳下阿蒙

wú xià ā méng

長江下游南岸的呂蒙；泛指人學識尚淺。

三國時的東吳名將呂蒙，汝南富陂(今安徽阜陽西南)人。他年青的時候，愛習武功而不好讀書。後來，聽從孫權的勸告，努力攻讀史書、兵書，成為文武兼備，果斷有膽的名將。

魯肅有時和他議論文韜武略時，竟然辯不過他。有一次，魯肅辯不過他時，忍不住拍著他的背說："我過去說你只曉武略，如今你卻學識英博，非復吳下阿蒙了。"

出自《三國志》

Lu Meng in the Kingdom of Wu

Said in reference to someone who has little learning.

During the Three Kingdoms Period, there was a famous general in the kingdom of Wu named Lu Meng. He lived in Fupi (in the southwest of present-day Fuyang, Anhui Province) in Runan Prefecture on the south bank of the lower reaches of the Yangtze River. When he was young he liked to practice with weapons and disliked to study. Later, he accepted Sun Quan's advice and began studying historical records and books on the art of war. He finally became a brave general, well-educated and trained in the art of war.

One day when Lu Su was discussing literature and military strategy with Lu Meng, Lu Meng got the better of the argument. Lu Su then said to Lu Meng, with admiration, "In the past, I thought you only knew about military strategy, but now I find you have great learning. So, you are not the former Lu Meng."

History of the Three Kingdoms

別開生面

bié kāi shēng miàn

另外創造新面貌；形容開創新風格、新形式。

曹霸是唐朝的著名畫家，被封為左武衛將軍，擅長畫馬和肖像。當時的畫馬名家韓幹和陳閎都拜他為師。天寶年間，唐玄宗召他畫‘御馬’和重新描繪《淩煙閣功臣像》。曹霸日以繼夜地作色和修復功臣像。完工後，唐玄宗大加讚賞。詩人杜甫也贈了一首詩給他：“淩煙功臣少顏色，將軍下筆開生面。”

出自《丹青引》

Opening Up a Fresh Look

Said of creating new styles and new forms.

Cao Ba was a famous painter of the Tang Dynasty and was skilled at painting horses and portraits. He was granted the title of Left Guard General. Han Gan and Chen Hong, also skillful at painting horses, both took Cao Ba as their teacher. During the Tianbao reign, Emperor Xuanzong summoned Cao Ba to paint "imperial horses" and repaint the portraits of meritorious statesmen and generals in the Lingyan Pavilion. Cao Ba worked day in and day out, and his work was highly appreciated by Emperor Xuanzong. The poet Du Fu wrote: "*The pictures and portraits in the Lingyan Pavilion were old and faded, The new ones repainted by the general now have a fresh look.*"

Collection of Paintings

坐山觀虎鬥

zuò shān guān hǔ dòu

坐在山上看兩虎相鬥；比喻觀望別人相鬥，伺機從中取利。

有一天，卞莊子在山頭望見兩隻老虎困住一頭牛。卞莊子想拔劍殺虎，館豎子阻止他說："兩虎都想食牛，一定會引起爭奪，相爭必會相鬥，相鬥必是強者傷，弱者死。到時你刺死傷虎，就有一舉殺兩虎之名了。"卞莊子覺得有理，於是靜觀其變。不一會兒，兩虎果然鬥了起來，結果一死一傷。卞莊子一劍刺死傷虎，成就了一舉殺兩虎之功了。

出自《史記》

Sitting on Top of the Mountain to Watch the Tigers Fight

Two Dogs Fight for a Bone, and a Third Runs Away with It

Said of people who watch in safety while others fight, then reap the spoils when both sides are exhausted.

One day Bian Zhuangzi saw two tigers cornering an ox. Bian wanted to kill the tigers with his sword, but Guan Shuzi stopped him, saying, "Both tigers want to eat the ox. So, they will fight for it, and, in the fight, the stronger one will be wounded and the weaker one will be killed. You can kill the wounded one with your sword, then you'll enjoy a good reputation for killing two tigers at one time." Bian thought it was reasonable, so he sat quietly biding his time. Soon, the two tigers began to fight. At last one was wounded and the other died. Bian killed the wounded one, and did win a reputation for killing two tigers at one time.

Records of the Historian

坐懷不亂

zuò huái bù luàn

美女坐在懷裡而不淫亂；比喻內心純潔，男女關係光明正大。

春秋時，魯國大夫柳下惠，有一天夜裡在郭門住宿。有一女子找不到住處，前來求宿。柳下惠答應了她的要求，而且見她衣衫單薄，惟恐夜寒把她凍死，於是解開外衣，讓她坐在懷裡，用外衣裹緊，兩人同坐一夜，並沒有非禮的行為。後來，柳下惠被稱為有女坐懷而不亂的正人君子。

出自《荀子》

坐懷不亂

Not Disturbed with a Pretty Woman in One's Lap

Used in reference to someone who is pure at heart, or when relations between the sexes are pure and innocent.

One evening during the Spring and Autumn Period, Liu Xiahui, a senior official of the state of Lu, spent the night at a city gate. When a pretty young woman arrived there and couldn't find accommodations for the night, she asked Liu if she could stay with him. Liu agreed, and when he saw that the woman wore thin clothes he let her sit in his lap and covered her with his overcoat. They sat there like that for the entire night. Of course, Liu did not engage in indecorous behavior. Later, he was known as an upright person who was not disturbed by having a woman in his lap all night.

The Book of Xun Zi

兵不厭詐

bīng bù yàn zhà

用兵作戰時，儘量使用假象來迷惑敵人。

東漢時，羌軍圍攻武都郡，安帝命虞詡為武都太守，率軍抗敵。虞詡的部隊行軍途中，被羌兵圍阻。虞詡見敵強我弱，不能硬闖，便放出消息說原地不動，等候援軍。羌人不知有詐，放任軍隊四處搶掠，軍紀渙散。虞詡見羌軍防線鬆懈，迅速突圍而出，日夜兼程，每天行軍一百多里。而且命士兵第一天挖兩個飯灶，以後逐日增加一倍。羌兵見天天增灶，以為虞詡的兵力日增，援軍已到，便不敢再追趕，虞詡帶領軍隊安抵武都郡了。

出自《後漢書》

Nothing Is Too Deceitful in War

All's Fair in Love and War

Said of creating false impressions to mislead the enemy.

During the Eastern Han Dynasty, when the Qiang army attacked Wudu Emperor Andi appointed Yu Xu prefect of Wudu and ordered him to lead an army to resist the invaders. Yu Xu's troops were besieged by the Qiang army on the way. Realizing that the enemy was stronger than his army, Yu Xu decided not to force the fight. Instead he ordered his troops to spread the word that they would stop marching and wait for the arrival of relief troops. The Qiang commander believed this rumor and let his troops go looting far and near. Taking advantage of the enemy's slackened discipline Yu Xu and his troops managed to break out of the encirclement. Marching at a speed of more than fifty kilometers a day, Yu Xu ordered his men to leave behind more field stoves each day to give the enemy the impression that he was constantly getting reinforcements. So, the enemy dared not pursue and attack his troops, and Yu Xu was able to lead his men safely to Wudu.

History of the Later Han Dynasty

兵貴神速

bīng guì shén sù

用兵貴在行動極為迅速；比喻辦事情重在迅速行動，切忌拖泥帶水。

三國時，曹操親自率兵征討袁熙、袁尚及北方三郡。曹軍兵馬、軍事物資太多，以致行軍緩慢。謀臣郭嘉對曹操說："用兵貴在神速。今千里進襲敵人，物資太多，難以行軍，對方容易探悉我軍動靜，必有防備。不如把大量物資留下，改派輕兵兼程趕路，出其不意地殺他個措手不及。"曹操採用了郭嘉的建議，率領數千精兵突擊敵軍心腹之地。袁熙、袁尚心慌意亂，趕忙逃跑了。

出自《三國志》

兵貴神速

Speed Is What Counts in War

Said of doing things deftly, not sloppily.

During the Three Kingdoms Period, Cao Cao led his troops on a punitive expedition against Yuan Xi and Yuan Shang and the three prefectures in the north. Cao's army was weighted down with many horses and much military material so the troops had to march slowly. Guo Jia, Cao Cao's councilor, said to Cao Cao, "Speed is what counts in war. We have marched five hundred kilometers to attack the enemy. It is difficult to press forward with so much equipment. If we march slowly, the enemy will learn of our operation and surely they will be prepared for us. It would be better to leave behind most of our supplies and dispatch lightly equipped troops. We'll then launch a surprise attack." Cao Cao adopted Guo Jia's suggestion and led several thousand picked troops to attack the enemy. Yuan Xi and Yuan Shang were so frightened that they fled pell-mell.

History of the Three Kingdoms

我醉欲眠

wǒ zuì yù mián

我醉了，想睡覺；指為人真誠坦率。

陶潛是東晉時的傑出詩人。他為人高潔，卑視官場穢弊。他任彭澤令時，因不屑巴結官吏，辭職不幹。後來，雖然受到徵召，但他再不為官，從此歸隱田園。他待人真誠，不論富人、窮人來探訪他，都設酒款待。如果他先喝醉了，便對客人說："我醉了，想睡覺，請你走吧。"人們都讚他性情真率如此，從不矯情造作。

出自《宋書》

I Am Drunk and Want to Sleep

Said of people who are sincere and frank.

Tao Qian, a famous poet of the Eastern Jin Dynasty, was a noble-minded man and hated the immoral conduct of officials. When he took office as the magistrate of Pengze, he hated to be obsequious to his superiors, so he resigned. Later, though he was again offered an official position, he refused to accept it. He went back to his hometown and began to live in seclusion, but was sincere with everyone. When people, rich or poor, came to visit him, he entertained them with wine. When he was drunk, he would say to his guests, "I am drunk. I want to sleep. Please go home." People all appreciated his frankness. He never tried to deceive others by covering up his real purpose.

Book of the Song Dynasty

我見猶憐

wǒ jiàn yóu lián

我見了尚且覺得可愛；形容女子姿態妙曼，楚楚動人。

東晉時，桓溫平蜀後，納了李勢的妹為妾。桓溫的妻子性情兇悍，知此事後，她怒氣沖天地拿著刀子走向李女的屋子，便想一刀殺了。當她走進房間時，見到正在梳頭的李女在結好頭髮後，便向她施禮。她看到李女姿貌清麗，神色閑正，言辭淒惋，頓時於心不忍，扔了刀子，抱住李女說："我見了你尚且覺得動人，何況那老匹夫！"

出自《世說新語》

When I See Her, Even I Cannot Help Loving Her

Said of women who are pretty and charming.

During the Eastern Jin Dynasty, after Huan Wen conquered Shu, he took Li Shi's younger sister as his concubine. Huan Wen's wife was ferocious and tough. After hearing the news, her anger was brought to a high pitch. Holding a knife, she ran to the girl's room, planning to kill her. When she entered the room, she saw the girl combing her hair. The girl tied up her hair, and then saluted her a bow. When she saw the beauty of the girl and her noble and graceful manner, she threw the knife down and gave the girl a big hug, saying, "On seeing you, even I, let alone the old scoundrel, my husband, feel you are lovely and touching."

New Social Anecdotes

改過自新

gǎi guò zì xīn

改正過錯，重新做人。

西漢名醫淳于意，精通望、聞、問、切四診，其中以望診、切診為著稱。有一次，因拒絕為權貴治病，被誣告下獄。幼女緹縈救父心切，上書漢文帝說："人死了不可復生，受刑的人被砍掉手腳不會復原。雖然想改過自新，也無補於事了。"她懇求漢文帝讓她代父受過。漢文帝被她的孝心感動，召見了她，赦免了淳于意。

出自《史記》

改過自新

Correct One's Errors and Start Anew

Turn Over a New Leaf

Said of mending one's ways and making a fresh start.

Chunyu Yi, a famous doctor of the Western Han Dynasty, was proficient in the four traditional methods of diagnosis—observation, auscultation and olfaction, interrogation, and pulse-taking and palpation. Once, he was accused falsely and sent to jail for refusing to cure the illnesses of influential officials. Ti Ying, his little daughter, was anxious to save her father. She submitted a written statement to Emperor Wendi, saying, "A dead man cannot be restored to life. If a prisoner is punished by cutting off his limbs, he will never be fully restored. Though he wants to correct his errors and make a fresh start, he can do nothing." She begged to bear the blame for her father. Deeply moved by her love for her father, Emperor Wendi granted an audience to Ti Ying, then set Chunyu Yi free.

Records of the Historian

長袖善舞

cháng xiù shàn wǔ

長衣袖，善於起舞；比喻有所憑借，做事容易成功；也形容有錢財、有手段的人善於鑽營。

戰國時期，范睢和蔡澤是著名的人物。他們都很有辯才，先後當過秦國的宰相。

范睢原是魏國人，後來，他來到齊國。齊襄王聽說他能言善辯，想用錢財換取魏國的機密，范睢堅拒不說，備受折磨，後裝死逃出，來到秦國，化名為張祿。他多次游説秦王採遠交近攻之策。秦昭王封他為宰相，一次因圍攻趙國邯鄲失敗，自請免相。

蔡澤原是燕國人，雄辯滔滔，曾游説各諸侯，但不被重用。他於是跑到秦國，被秦昭王召見，並拜為客卿。後繼范雎為宰相。

范、蔡二人先後拜相，史學家司馬遷説："韓子説'長袖善舞，多錢善賈'這話不由不信。范雎、蔡澤就憑著辯才過人而拜相。"

出自《史記》

Skillful at Dancing with Long Sleeves

Said of persons who are given assistance and do things easily, or who have money and property and by tricks secure personal gain.

Fan Ju and Cai Ze were famous in the Warring States Period, and both were quite eloquent and had been the prime minister of the state of Qin.

Originally, Fan Ju lived in the state of Wei, and later came to the state of Qi. When King Xiang of Qi learned of Fan Ju's eloquence he wanted to win him over. He gave money to Fan to gain the secrets of Wei. But Fan refused to say anything, and so he was severely tortured. Later, he escaped from Qi and came to Qin, going by the name of Zhang Lu. He convinced the king of Qin to keep friendly relations with distant states and attack those nearby. King Zhao of Qin then granted him the title of prime minister. Once, Zhang led troops to attack Handan in the state of Zhao, but Zhang's troops were defeated and he asked the king to relieve him from his post.

Originally, Cai Ze lived in the state of Yan. He had a silver tongue and went about selling his ideas everywhere. But no one would give him an important position. So he left Yan, and went to Qin. King Zhao of Qin called him in and asked him to be his *keqing* (a person from one feudal state serving in the court of another). Following Fan Ju, he became prime minister. Sima Qian, the great historian, said, "Han Fei Zi once said, 'It is true that if you have long sleeves, you'll be good at dancing; if you have much money, you'll be good at business.' Fan Ju and Cai Ze became prime minister because both of them have the gift of the gab."

Records of the Historian

沾沾自喜

zhān zhān zì xǐ

自以為不錯而得意；對自己的成績感覺得意，現出輕浮的樣子。

漢景帝時，劉濞勾結六個諸侯國，發動‘吳楚七國之亂’。景帝任命竇嬰為大將軍，平定叛亂。竇嬰平亂有功，被封為魏其侯，威望漸盛。丞相劉舍因庸碌無能而被免職，竇太后提議讓竇嬰繼任。漢景帝不同意，說：“竇嬰這人，常自以為是而沾沾自喜，辦事草率輕浮，難以為相。”竇嬰直至漢武帝劉徹即位後才得以為相。

出自《史記》

Being Pleased with Oneself

Said of people who are complacent over an occasional success, and behave frivolously.

During the reign of Emperor Jingdi of the Han Dynasty, Liu Bi conspired with six princely states in a seven-state rebellion. Emperor Jingdi appointed Dou Ying senior general and ordered him to suppress the rebellion, and Dou Ying succeeded in so doing. The emperor then granted him the title of Marquis of Weiqi. Gradually, his prestige became greater and greater. Liu She, the prime minister, was removed from office because he was mediocre and incompetent, and Empress Dowager Dou suggested that Dou Ying take his place. Emperor Jingdi disagreed with her, saying, "Dou Ying can't be prime minister because he considers himself always in the right. He is always pleased with himself, and behaves frivolously." Later, Dou Ying became prime minister during the reign of Emperor Wudi of the Han Dynasty.

Records of the Historian

兩袖清風

liǎng xiù qīng fēng

兩袖迎風飄盪；現多形容為政清廉或沒有財產，生活貧寒。

于謙是明朝傑出的政治家、軍事家。他為官廉潔，平反冤獄，救災賑荒，受到百姓擁護。明宣宗時，宦官王振專權，貪污腐化。外地官員進京，都要向他獻上財帛、珠寶。有一次，于謙入京辦事，有人勸他送些土特產給王振，搞好關係。于謙聽後，仰天大笑，揮筆寫詩："絹帕麻菇與線香，本資民用反為殃，清風兩袖朝天去，免得閭閻話短長。"

出自《入京》詩

兩袖清風

Two Sleeves Flapping in the Wind

Used in reference to people who are upright and just, or who have no property and live a poor life.

Yu Qian was a prominent statesman and strategist who was honest in performing his official duties. He did many good things for people, such as redressing injustices and providing disaster relief, and the people supported him. During the reign of Emperor Xuanzong of the Ming Dynasty, Wang Zhen, a eunuch, was imperious, despotic, and corrupt. When officials from other places came to the capital, they would present him with money and jewelry. Once, when Yu Qian went to the capital, someone advised him to bring Wang Zhen some special local products. Yu Qian laughed sardonically and wrote a poem at once, "*Silk, cloth, linen, mushrooms and other things were originally daily necessities, But now all these things are used as bribes. I will leave this world with nothing but wind in my sleeves, To avoid becoming the talk of the street!"*

Entering the Capital

盲人瞎馬

máng rén xiā mǎ

盲人騎瞎馬；比喻處境非常危險或指魯莽行事，後果嚴重。

顧愷之是東晉傑出的畫家，而且擅長詩賦和書法，有‘才絕、畫絕、癡絕’之稱。他經常和桓玄、殷仲堪等朋友談天說地。有一天，他們約定作‘危語’，即用一句說話形容十分危險的情況。桓玄說：“矛頭淅米劍頭炊（把矛槍和劍頭當米煮飯吃）。”殷仲堪說：“百歲老翁攀枯枝。”顧愷之說：“井上轆轤臥嬰兒。”這時剛好有個軍官在座，插話說：“盲人騎瞎馬，夜半臨深池。”殷仲堪聽了說：“這實在是危險！”顧愷之、桓玄等人望著他笑。原來殷仲堪有一隻眼是瞎的。

出自《世說新語》

A Blind Man on a Blind Horse

Used in reference to someone who is in a dangerous situation or who acts rashly.

Gu Kaizhi was an outstanding painter of the Eastern Jin Dynasty. He was also a skillful poet and calligrapher, and described by his contemporaries as "peerless in talent, painting, and imagination." He often chatted with Huan Xuan, Yin Zhongkan, and other friends. One day, when they gathered, they agreed to go in for a "word game," whereby each of them should say something to describe danger. Huan Xuan said, "Cook spearheads and swordheads as food for dinner." Yin Zhongkan said, "A centenarian is climbing a withered tree." Gu Kaizhi said, "A baby is sleeping on a well-pulley." An army officer chipped in, "A blind man riding a blind horse past a deep ditch at midnight." Yin Zhongkan exclaimed, "That's really very dangerous!" Looking at him, Gu Kaizhi, Huan Xuan, and others laughed because Yin was blind in one eye.

New Social Anecdotes

青雲直上

qīng yún zhí shàng

沖著青天上升；比喻地位、名望直線上升。

范雎是戰國時期的魏國人，齊襄王利誘他出賣魏國的機密，他堅拒不從，被拷打折磨，裝死逃回魏國，魏國大夫須賈懷疑他私通齊國。范雎後來到了秦國，改名為張祿，於秦昭王四十一年拜相。有一次，秦國攻打魏國，須賈到秦國求和。范雎穿著破衣和須賈相見，須賈見他潦倒貧困，可憐兮兮，請他吃飯，並送了一件袍子給他。須賈想求見秦相張祿，范雎說可以引見。兩人到了相府，須賈等候召見。可是范雎進了相府後，過了很久還沒有消息。須賈向侍者打聽動靜，侍者說范雎就是張祿。須賈大驚，趕忙磕頭跪爬到堂前對范雎說："我犯了死罪，意想不到您能自致青雲之上。"

出自《史記》

Soaring High into the Clouds

Said of people who are promoted to ever-higher posts and enjoy ever-greater fame and prestige.

Fan Ju lived in the state of Wei during the Warring States Period. King Xiang of Qi tried to tempt him to reveal Wei's secrets, but Fan refused to say anything and suffered severe torture. He eventually escaped from Qi and returned to Wei. Xu Jia, a senior Wei official, was suspicious of Fan Ju, and thought that Fan Ju might be in secret communication with Qi. Later, Fan Ju came to Qin, going by the name of Zhang Lu. In the forty-first year of the reign of King Zhao of Qin, Fan Ju became prime minister. When Qin attacked Wei, Xu Jia was sent to Qin to sue for peace. Fan Ju, wearing old clothes, met Xu Jia there. Seeing that Fan Ju was penniless and frustrated, Xu Jia invited him to dinner and gave him a cotton-padded robe. Xu Jia asked to see Zhang Lu, the prime minister, but Fan Ju made him wait. Fan Ju entered the residence of the prime minister as Xiu Jia waited and waited for a long time. When Xu Jia asked an attendant what was going on, the attendant said that Fan Ju was actually Zhang Lu, the prime minister. Hearing this, Xu Jia was greatly surprised. He hurriedly crawled into the hall, knelled, and begged for a pardon, saying to Fan Ju, "I am sorry. I have committed a capital crime. I didn't expect to find you soaring high into the clouds."

Records of the Historian

金屋藏嬌

jīn wū cáng jiāo

用金屋藏住阿嬌；比喻另築愛巢與情婦同居。

漢武帝劉徹在幾歲大的時候，他的姑母劉嫖抱他坐在膝上，問道：“你想要妻子嗎？”他說：“想妻子。”劉嫖於是指著左右百多個宮女，讓他挑選。但劉徹一個也看不上眼。最後，劉嫖指住自已的愛女，問：“阿嬌好不好？”劉徹笑著拍掌說：“好！若得阿嬌為妻，一定築金屋，藏阿嬌。”

出自《漢武故事》

金屋藏嬌

Keeping Ah Jiao in a Chamber of Gold

Used in reference to someone who keeps a mistress in a luxury abode.

When Liu Che, or Emperor Wudi of the Western Han Dynasty, was a little boy, one day his aunt Liu Piao carried him at her breast and asked, "Do you want to have a wife?" He replied, "Yes, I do." Liu Piao pointed to over one hundred maids in the palace asking, "Who do you want?" The little boy held them all in contempt. At last, Liu Piao pointed to her daughter, asking, "Is Ah Jiao lovely?" Liu Che clapped his hands and replied, "If Ah Jiao will be my wife, I will have a chamber of gold built for her."

Story of Emperor Wudi of the Han Dynasty

金剛怒目

jīn gāng nù mù

四大金剛瞪著眼睛；形容儀容威武，使人望而生畏。

隋朝的時候，有一天，吏部侍郎薛道衡到鍾山開善寺遊玩。他故意考問一個小僧人："金剛為甚麼怒目而視，菩薩卻又為何低眉？"小僧人不慌不忙地回答："金剛怒目，所以降伏四魔；菩薩低眉，所以慈悲六道。"薛道衡聽了，一時無言以對。

出自《太平廣記》

Glaring Like a Vajra

Said of a powerful, awe-inspiring appearance.

One day during the Sui Dynasty, Xue Daoheng, Vice-Minister of Personnel, went to the Kaishan Temple on Zhongshan Mountain. While there he questioned a little monk, "Why do the vajras warriors glare, while the Buddha looks serene?" The little monk answered unhurriedly, "The vajras (guardian warriors) glare so they can conquer the four monsters; the Buddha lowers his eyebrows for six merciful dispensations." Hearing this, Xue Daoheng had nothing to say for the moment.

Stories Compiled in the Taiping Period

狐死首丘

hú sǐ shǒu qiū

狐狸死的時候，頭向著狐穴所在的土丘；比喻懷念故鄉，不忘本。

據説，土丘是狐狸窟穴根本的所在地，儘管狐狸死得如何狼狠，頭部的方向總要向著狐穴所在的土丘。

出自《禮記》

A Fox Dies with Its Face Toward Its Den

Said of someone longing for home or mindful of his origin.

It is said that earth mounds are the locations of foxes' caves. No matter how they die, their heads always point toward the earth mounds.

The Book of Rites

枕戈待旦

zhěn gē dài dàn

枕著兵器，等待天亮；形容殺敵心切，一刻也不鬆懈。

西晉將軍、詩人劉琨，年青時與祖逖等人為友，他們都想為國家幹一番事業。有一天，他聽説好友祖逖被朝廷錄用，心裡非常焦急，寫信給親屬説："我每天枕戈待旦，期待殺敵報國，可是祖逖先我去建功立業了。"後來，劉琨在二十六歲的時候，也被朝廷錄用了。

出自《晉書》

Sleep on One's Spear Till Daybreak

Said of being eager to kill the enemy, not relaxing for a moment.

Liu Kun, a general of the Western Jin Dynasty, was also a poet who became friends with Zu Ti. They both wanted to do something for the country. One day, hearing that his good friend Zu Ti was employed by the imperial court, Liu Kun felt very anxious and wrote to a relative, "I sleep on my spear till dawn every day, wishing to kill the enemy and serve the country worthily. However, Zu Ti will render meritorious service before I get the chance." Later, at the age of twenty-six, Liu

Kun was also employed by the imperial court.

History of the Jin Dynasty

杵臼之交

chǔ jiù zhī jiāo

結交於棒槌和石臼之間；比喻交友不嫌貧賤、出身。

東漢時，有個貧寒、好學的讀書人叫公沙穆。他很想入太學深造，但苦無資糧。於是，他打扮成傭工的樣子，到富戶吳祐家裡當舂米工掙錢入學。有一天，公沙穆正在舂米，吳祐來到，與他攀談起來。言談間，吳祐驚奇公沙穆知書識禮，學問淵博。兩人越談越投契，便在杵臼之間結交為好朋友。

出自《後漢書》

Making Friends by the Pestle and Mortar

Said of making true friends, regardless of their poor or humble family background.

In the Eastern Han Dynasty there was a poor but studious man named Gong Shamu. He wanted to enter the Imperial College for further study, but suffered from lack of money and food. So, dressed like a hired laborer, he hulled rice for Wu You to earn enough money to enter college. One day, Wu You came by while Gong Shamu was hulling the rice and began to chitchat with him. During this conversation, Wu You was surprised at Gong Shamu's profound knowledge and sensibility. The two men had a congenial talk, and made friends with each other while standing by the pestle and mortar.

History of the Later Han Dynasty

杳如黃鶴

yǎo rú huáng hè

像黃鶴一樣，不見蹤影；比喻一去就無影無蹤，下落不明。

從前，有一個叫荀瓌的人，有一天他在黃鶴樓遊玩休憩，忽然望見西南面有物從雲霄飄然而降，瞬息間已到樓上，原來是個駕鶴的仙人。荀瓌和仙人對飲，歡談暢快。不久，仙人告辭，跨鶴騰空，消失在雲端之間，見不到蹤影了。

出自《述異記》

Disappearing Like the Yellow Crane

Said of someone who vanishes and whose whereabouts remain a mystery.

Once upon a time, there lived a man named Xun Gui. One day he visited the Huanghe (Yellow Crane) Tower and took a rest there. Suddenly he saw something coming down from the clouds in the southwest, and it arrived at the tower in the twinkling of an eye. It was an immortal riding a crane. Xun Gui drank and talked with the immortal freely and to their hearts' content. Soon after, the immortal left. He rose up into the sky, riding the crane, and disappeared between the clouds.

Strange Tales

披荊斬棘

pī jīng zhǎn jí

劈開荊枝，砍斷棘木；比喻清除障礙，克服困難，開闢道路。

馮異是東漢初期的將領，幫助劉秀爭天下。劉秀即位後，每當諸將並坐論功時，他總是退避樹下，從不爭功，軍中稱為‘大樹將軍’。後來，劉秀封他為陽夏侯，任征西大將軍。有一年，馮異到京師朝拜，漢光帝劉秀對文武百官說：“馮異是我起兵時的主簿，為我披荊斬棘，平定了關中，立下許多戰功。”

出自《後漢書》

披荊斬棘

Hacking Through Brambles and Thistles

Said of clearing away obstacles in one's way.

Feng Yi, a general of the early Eastern Han Dynasty, helped Liu Xiu fight for the founding of the dynasty. After Liu Xiu ascended the throne, whenever the generals sat together discussing their rewards, Feng Yi always kept out of the way under a tree, never fighting for honors, and so was called "the General under the Tree." Later he was granted the title Marquis of Yangxia by Liu Xiu, and appointed the Great General for Western Expedition. One year, when Feng Yi went to the capital to pay respects to Liu Xiu, the Emperor said to his civil and military officers, "Feng Yi was the Keeper of the Records when I revolted. He hacked through brambles and thistles for my sake, pacified the Central Shaanxi Plain, and rendered many meritorious military services."

History of the Later Han Dynasty

抱殘守缺

bào cán shǒu quē

保守住殘缺陳舊的東西；形容因循守舊，不肯接受新事物。

劉歆是西漢時的經學家、數學家，曾設計統一全國度量衡制的圓柱形標準量器，由規定的面積和直徑求出圓周率是三點一五四七。劉歆少時好學，精通詩書、典籍。有一次，他在古書堆中發現了一本古文《春秋左氏傳》。劉歆非常高興，向朝廷建議設立古籍學官，但受到一些大官反對，劉歆很氣憤的說：“這些人抱殘守缺，只會抱住陳舊的東西，不肯探求新的知識。”

出自《漢書》

Clinging to the Broken and Outworn

Said of continuing in the same old rut, unwilling to accept new things.

Liu Xin was a Confucianist and mathematician during the Western Han Dynasty. He designed a cylindrical standard measure which unified national measurements and calculated the ratio of the circumference of a circle to its diameter at 3.1547, or pi. Liu Xin was studious as a young man and proficient in poetry and ancient learning. Once, when he discovered *Zuo Qiuming's Chronicles* among some ancient books, Liu Xin was very pleased and suggested that the court establish a scholar for ancient books. However, some powerful officials opposed him. Liu Xin said indignantly, "These people cling only to the broken and outworn things, unwilling to seek new knowledge."

History of the Han Dynasty

居安思危

jū ān sī wēi

在安定的時候，要思慮可能會出現的危機與災難。

春秋時期，鄭國為了擴張勢力，欺負弱小的宋國。強大的楚國、晉國聯合各國反對鄭國。鄭國驚慌起來，派使者到楚國求和，但楚國不予理會。鄭國再派使者到晉國求和、歸順，並送了很多禮物給晉悼公。晉悼公答應了與鄭國和解。晉悼公滿心歡喜，把禮物分贈給大臣。功臣魏絳直言說："我們應居安思危，思則有備，有備無患。"

出自《左傳》

Think of Danger While Living in Peace

Provide for a Rainy Day

Meaning one should be ever prepared for possible danger while enjoying a secure life.

During the Spring and Autumn Period, the Zheng State invaded the weak Song State in order to expand its power. The strong Chu and Jin then united other states to fight Zheng. Zheng was frightened by this and sent envoys to sue for peace with Chu, but Chu paid no attention to this. Zheng sent envoys again, this time to Jin to sue for peace and pledge their allegiance. They brought many gifts to Duke Dao of Jin, who agreed to make peace with Zheng and happily presented the gifts to the ministers. Wei Jiang, a general who had rendered outstanding service, said frankly, "We should be mindful of danger in times of peace. Keeping this in mind, we will be able to avert peril."

Zuo Qiuming's Chronicles

明鏡高懸

míng jìng gāo xuán

高高掛起明察善惡的鏡子；比喻執法者公正嚴明。

傳說秦始皇有一面鏡子，闊四尺，高五尺九寸。如果掩著心來照這面鏡子，就會知道患了甚麼病。這面鏡子還有一樣神奇之處，但凡女子存有不軌之心，被鏡子一照，就會心驚肉跳。所以，秦始皇經常用這面鏡子來照宮女，一旦發現有異常反應，就把她殺掉。

出自《西京雜記》

明鏡高懸

A Bright Mirror Hanging High

Meaning a clear mirror hanging high above a person's head enables him to make a clear distinction between the ugly and the beautiful, the evil and the good. Also said of law executors who are just, strict, and impartial.

According to legend, Emperor Qin Shi Huang had a mirror with a width of 1.22 by 1.75 meters. People could discover the nature of their disease when they looked at themselves in the mirror while covering their heart. The mirror had another magical function: If a woman cherished evil designs, she would shudder with fear when facing it. Therefore, the Emperor often ordered the maids in the imperial palace to face the mirror. Whenever he found something unusual in a woman, he would get rid of her.

Miscellaneous Notes of the Western Capital

首尾相應

shǒu wěi xiāng yìng

頭和尾相互接應；形容作戰、工作時各部分互相接應和支援；也形容文章、詩詞結構嚴謹。

孫武在論兵之道時說：“善於用兵的人，將軍隊佈陣成蛇一樣的陣式。因為蛇的頭部被攻擊，牠會用尾巴來反擊；如果尾部被攻擊，牠就用頭部來反擊；一旦腰部被攻擊，蛇的首尾同時還擊。這樣的陣式使軍隊成為一個整體，各部份能夠互相照應、互相救援。”

出自《孫子》

Head and Tail Correspond with Each Other

Said when all parts correspond with and assist each other; also refering to well-knit essays and poems.

Sun Wu said while talking about military strategies, "Those who are good at commanding troops marshal their soldiers in ranks shaped like a snake when ready for battle. For a snake will strike back with its tail if its head is attacked; and it will strike back with its head if its tail is attacked, and strike back with both head and tail at the same time if its middle is attacked. In this formation the troops become a complete entirety, and each part can correspond with and support the other parts."

The Book of Sun Zi

神機妙算

shén jī miào suàn

神奇的機智，巧妙的籌謀；形容機智過人，不可測度。

三國時，曹操率十萬大軍攻打劉備和孫權。劉備派諸葛亮聯合孫權共同對敵。諸葛亮答應周瑜三天內交出十萬枝箭的任務，並且立下軍令狀，到期不交，斬首示眾。諸葛亮向魯肅要了二十隻快船，每隻船上配三十名士兵，每隻船上紮了一千多個草人。等到第三天五更時分，趁著黎明前的大霧，諸葛亮下令快船向曹軍的水寨迫近，詐攻曹軍。曹操不知虛實，下令一萬多弓箭手向江中射箭。等到旭日初昇，諸葛亮下令各船迅速回航。二十隻船上的草人都掛滿了箭枝，已經超過十萬之數了。

魯肅把諸葛亮草船借箭的妙計告訴了周瑜，周瑜大驚，雖然平日嫉恨諸葛亮，也不禁慨然嘆息說："諸葛亮神機妙算，我不如他。"

出自《三國演義》

Clever Strategy and Shrewd Tactics

Said of people who are unusually quick-witted.

During the Three Kingdoms Period, Cao Cao led one hundred thousand troops to attack Liu Bei and Sun Quan. Liu Bei assigned Zhuge Liang to unite with Sun Quan to oppose the attack. Zhuge Liang promised Zhou Yu that he would have one hundred thousand arrows ready for Zhou Yu in three days, and made a military pledge that if he could not accomplish this in time, Zhou Yu could cut off his head and display it in public. Zhuge Liang then asked Lu Su for twenty fast boats with thirty soldiers and over one thousand straw figures for each boat. They waited till the fifth watch of the third day, and taking advantage of the thick fog before daybreak, Zhuge Liang ordered the men to steer the boats near to Cao Cao's naval base for a feint attack. Cao Cao was unsure of the actual situation and ordered his men to shoot arrows at the approaching boats. When the sun rose early that morning, Zhuge Liang ordered the boat men to return immediately. The straw figures on the twenty boats were all covered with a total of one hundred thousand arrows.

When Lu Su told Zhou Yu about Zhuge Liang's marvelous plan of using straw figures on the boats to get the arrows from Cao Cao, Zhou Yu was shocked at this news. Though he hated Zhuge Liang out of jealousy, he could not help sighing, "Zhuge Liang used clever strategy and shrewd tactics, and I am not as good as he."

Tales of the Three Kingdoms

神機妙算

神龍見首不見尾

shén lóng jiàn shǒu bù jiàn wěi

只見龍頭，看不見龍尾；形容行蹤詭秘，難於捉摸。

清朝的時候，有一天，趙執信與洪升一同在王士禛的家裡論詩。洪升說："詩有如龍一樣，首、尾、爪、角、鱗、鬣，缺一不可，都不是龍，也就不成詩。"王士禛不同意他的論點，說："詩猶如神龍，見其首不見其尾，或在雲中露出一爪一鱗而已，怎麼會得全體？"

出自《談龍錄》

The Head of the Magic Dragon Is Visible and Its Tail Invisible

Said of people who are unfathomable and secret in their movements.

One day during the Qing Dynasty, Zhao Zhixin and Hong Sheng were commenting on some poems at Wang Shizhen's house. Hong Sheng said, "A poem is like a dragon. Without the head, tail, claws, horns, scales, or hair, it would not be a dragon; the same is true of a poem." Wang Shizhen disagreed with him, saying, "A poem is like a magic dragon, whose head is visible, but whose tail is invisible, or who reveals only one of its claws or scales through the clouds. How can you see it completely?"

Records of Dragons

亭亭玉立

tíng tíng yù lì

形容身材修長而秀麗的年輕女子；也形容花木形體挺拔勻稱。

北齊時期的武成帝高湛，因酒色過度，弄至精神恍惚，終於病倒了。他召當時有名的醫學家徐之才替他看病。他神情古怪的對徐之才說：“有一次，我如夢如幻般看見空中懸著一個五色物體，好奇之下，稍為走近前看，那個五色物體忽然間變成了一個絕色美人，離地數丈，亭亭玉立，好看極了！”徐之才聽了，搖搖頭，唯有替他調治病情。

出自《北齊書》

亭亭玉立

Standing Gracefully Erect

Said of young women who are slim and beautiful; and of flowers and trees which are tall, straight, and well-balanced.

During the Northern Qi Dynasty, Emperor Wuchengdi (Gao Zhan) often went about with a wandering mind and finally had to keep to his bed due to over-indulgence in wine and women. He asked Xu Zhicai, a famous doctor of the time, to cure his disease. The emperor said to Xu Zhicai with a strange expression on his face, "Once I saw as if I were dreaming of a colorful object hanging in the air. Curious, I drew nearer to look at it. It suddenly turned into an exceedingly beautiful lady, dozens of feet from the ground, standing gracefully erect. How pretty she was!" Hearing this, Xu Zhicai shook his head, and began to cure the emperor with his medical treatment.

History of the Northern Qi Dynasty

枯樹生花

kū shù shēng huā

枯萎的樹又開花；比喻絕處逢生，重獲新機。

古時候，有一個人，好求道術而不知求道的方法。但他日夜跪拜一棵枯樹，祈求長生不老，如此堅持了二十八年。有一天，枯樹忽然間開了花，花汁甜蜜。有人教他把花及花汁一起服食。他服用後，立即成了仙。

出自《續博物誌》

A Withered Tree Brings Forth Flowers

Said of people who are snatched from the jaws of death, and get new opportunities.

In ancient times, there was a man who worshipped Taoism but did not know how to seek Tao (the Way). He kowtowed to a withered tree day and night, praying to be ever-young. He persisted in doing this for twenty-eight years, before, one day, the withered tree suddenly brought forth flowers with sweet juice. He was told to consume the flowers and juice together. He did so, and became an immortal immediately.

Notes on the Investigation of Things

相提並論

xiāng tí bìng lùn

合併在一起談論；把不同的人或事合併，不加區別地一概而論。

有一年，漢景帝立栗太子，請竇嬰任太子的老師。幾年以後，漢景帝要廢栗太子，竇嬰多次奏請勸阻，引起景帝對他的不滿。竇嬰一氣之下，裝病不理朝廷事務。後來，許多人都勸竇嬰恢復入朝辦事，但都勸不動他。有一個叫高遂的人，勸竇嬰說：“能給你富貴的是主上，你是竇太后的侄子，竇太后和你親近。你是太子的老師，太子被廢掉，你無法挽回便裝病不辦事。你把這些事相提並論，是明顯地張揚主上的過失，不滿主上的決定啊！”竇嬰覺得高遂說的有理，便入朝辦事了。

出自《史記》

Mentioned in the Same Breath

Said of merging different people or things, and treating them as the same regardless of their differences.

One year, Emperor Jingdi of the Han Dynasty asked Dou Ying to teach the crown prince Li. Several years later, Emperor Jingdi wanted to depose the crown prince, but Dou Ying petitioned the Emperor to dissuade him from doing it, which made Emperor Jingdi resentful. Indignantly, Dou Ying pretended to be ill and would not attend to court affairs. Many people tried to persuade Dou Ying to resume court activities, but none succeeded in convincing him. A man named Gao Sui advised him, "The Emperor gave you wealth and honor. You are Empress Dowager Dou's nephew, and she is close to you, and you are the prince's teacher. The prince has been dethroned, and you cannot do anything about it, so you pretended to be ill and have stopped dealing with court affairs. In mentioning these things in the same breath, you obviously publicized His Majesty's faults and resented His Majesty's decisions!" Dou Ying felt Gao Sui's words reasonable, so he resumed court affairs.

Records of the Historian

相生相克

xiāng shēng xiāng kè

相互生發，相互克制；也指兩者互相依存，互相制約。

相生相克是五行家的學説。五行：金、木、水、火、土。相生：木生火、火生土、土生金、金生水、水生木。相克：木克土、土克水、水克火、火克金、金克木。

出自《説岳全傳》

Reinforcing and Counteracting Each Other

Used in reference to interdependent things which restrict and interact with each other.

This is a theory of the exponents of the Five Elements Doctrine. These five elements (gold, wood, water, fire, and earth) interact with each other: Fire comes from wood, earth comes from fire, gold from earth, water from gold, and wood from water. The five elements also restrict each other: Earth is restricted by wood, water by earth, fire by water, gold by fire, and wood by gold.

A Tale of Yue Fei

南山可移，判不可搖

nán shān kě yí, pàn bù kě yáo

終南山可移，判決不能動；指案件既經判定，絕不更改。

唐朝時，李元紘做雍州司戶。有一次，唐高宗與武則天的女兒太平公主，恃勢霸佔僧寺的磨房。案件交由李元紘審理，李元紘執法不阿，將磨房判還給僧寺。當時的太平公主權傾朝野，雍州長史竇懷貞懼怕太平公主的權勢，促令李元紘改判。李元紘不為所動，說："南山或可移，判不可搖！"

出自《新唐書》

Mt. Zhongnan Might Be Removed, But the Decision Might Not Be Removed

Used in reference to a settled case which cannot be changed.

During the Tang Dynasty, Li Yuanhong was the revenue manager of Yongzhou. Once Princess Taiping, daughter of Empress Wu Zetian and Emperor Gaozong, forcibly occupied the mill of a temple by taking advantage of her power. This case was tried by Li Yuanhong, who executed the law justly, and returned the mill to the temple. In fear of Princess Taiping's great power in the court, Dou Huaizhen, the prefect of Yongzhou, ordered Li Yuanhong to change his judgment. Li Yuanhong paid no attention to him, saying, "Mt. Zhongnan might be removed, but not this decision!"

New History of the Tang Dynasty

風吹草動

fēng chuī cǎo dòng

風輕輕一吹，草就搖動；比喻輕微的變化或動蕩。

春秋時期，楚國大夫伍奢因直言進諫，被楚平王所殺，大兒子伍尚也遭厄運。次子伍員(伍子胥)喬裝打扮，逃奔吳國。在逃亡生涯中，伍員晝伏夜出，偷蹤竊道，忍氣吞聲。一有風吹草動，便隱身藏形。當伍員來到昭關時，因守衛森嚴，無法通過。伍員找朋友東皋公幫助。但等了七天，還沒有出關的機會。伍員萬分焦慮，一夜之間，頭髮、鬍子全變白了。東皋公見此情況，提議他趁著鬍髮皆白，喬裝蒙混過關。伍員果然出了關口，繼續逃亡。

後來，伍員到了吳國，當了吳國的大夫。他幫助吳國整軍經武，不久率軍攻破了楚國。

出自《伍子胥變文》

The Grass Stirs When the Wind Blows

Said of a slight change or disturbance.

During the Spring and Autumn Period, Wu She, a senior official of the Chu State, was killed by King Ping because of his blunt criticism. His eldest son, Wu Shang, also suffered misfortune. Wu Yuan (Wu Zixu), his second son, disguised himself and fled to the Wu State. While fleeing, Wu Yuan went into hiding by day and came out at night, swallowing insults and humiliation silently. He would hide at the mere rustle of the grass in the wind. Wu Yuan could not get through Zhaoguan Pass because it was strongly guarded, so he asked his friend Dong Gaogong for help. But for seven days there was no opportunity for him to pass, and his hair and beard turned white with worries overnight. Seeing this, Dong Gaogong suggested he take advantage of his white hair and beard and disguise himself in order to slip by. In this way Wu Yuan was finally able to get to the Wu State.

After arriving in Wu, Wu Yuan became a minister there and helped Wu reorganize the army and strengthen its military power. Soon after, he led the Wu troops to conquer the Chu State.

Essays by Wu Zixu

信口雌黃

xìn kǒu cí huáng

胡說亂寫；比喻不顧事實、不負責任地亂說。

西晉時，有一個叫王衍的人，好談老莊義理。他在發表議論時，手執拂塵，不假思索，隨口就說，信口更改。當時的人寫字用黃紙，寫錯了就用雌黃塗了重寫。所以人們就諷刺他是‘信口雌黃’，亂說亂改。

出自《晉陽秋》

Loosening One's Tongue and Using Orpiment Freely

Shooting Off One's Mouth

Said of speaking loosely, heedless of the facts.

In the Western Jin Dynasty, there was a man named Wang Yan who was fond of discussing the philosophical doctrines of Zhuang Zi with his friends. He blurted out whatever came into his head, and changed his words whenever he liked, holding a horsetail whisk as was the Taoist custom. People at that time wrote on yellow paper, and whenever they wrote anything wrong, they used orpiment to erase it and rewrote. Therefore, people satirized him for making irresponsible remarks.

Records of Jinyang

後生可畏

hòu shēng kě wèi

年輕人值得敬畏；讚揚年輕人聰明努力，超越前輩。

有一次，孔子在遊學時，碰到一個小孩用泥土堆成一座城堡，坐在裡面不出來，也不給孔子讓路。孔子問他："你坐在裡面，為甚麼不避讓我的車子呢？"小孩回答說："只有車子繞城走，沒聽說過城堡要避車的。"孔子驚訝地說："小小年紀就懂得道理！"小孩又說："魚生下來，三天就會游泳；兔生下來，三天就能跑；馬生下來，三天就跟著母馬走。這些都是很自然的事，與大小有甚麼關係呢？"孔子由衷地說："後生可畏，焉知來者之不如今也。"

出自《論語》

後生可畏

The After-Born Should Be Regarded with Awe

Meaning young people should be respected, for they are bright, hard-working, and overreach their seniors.

While travelling to another state, Confucius saw a child sitting in a little castle he made from earth, and the child refused to make way for him. Confucius asked him, "Why don't you avoid my cart?" The child answered, "A cart can go around a castle. I have not heard that a castle should avoid a cart." Confucius said, surprised, "You are so little, yet you can understand this!" The child said, "Fish swim, rabbits run, horses follow their mothers three days after they are born. All this is very natural. Do these things matter whether they are big or small?" Confucius said sincerely, "An after-born should be regarded with awe. How can one say the younger generation is not as good as the old!"

Confucian Analects

飛短流長

fēi duǎn liú cháng

散佈是非；形容無中生有，造謠惑眾。

從前，有一美女范十一娘。有一年，在七月十五的廟會上，認識了一個和她一樣美艷的女子，叫封三娘。兩人越談越投契，臨別，范十一娘邀封三娘到她家裡玩，封三娘答應了。

可是一連過了幾個月，封三娘並沒出現，范十一娘因思念過度，病了起來。一天傍晚，范十一娘和婢女到花園玩，突然瞧見封三娘爬在牆上往園裡望。范十一娘喜出望外，拉著她進園，輕責她說："你為甚麼現在才來，想死人家啦。"封三娘說："我也很想念你，但我是貧窮人家，你是千金小姐。我與你交往，就怕造謠生事的人，飛短流長，使人不堪忍受。”范十一娘再也不讓她離開。自此，兩人形影不離，情如姊妹。原來，封三娘是狐狸變的。

出自《聊齋誌異》

Rumors and Gossip Travel Apace

Said of spreading embroidered stories and malicious gossip.

Once upon a time, there was a beauty named Fan Shiyiniang. At the July the Fifteenth Fair she met Feng Sanniang, a girl as beautiful as herself. They talked very congenially and Fan Shiyiniang invited Feng Sanniang to visit her house, and Feng Sanniang agreed.

Several months passed but Feng Sanniang did not appear. Fan Shiyiniang missed her very much and became ill. One evening, while playing in the garden with her maid, Fan Shiyiniang saw Feng Sanniang leaning over the wall, trying to look inside. Overjoyed, Fan Shiyiniang brought her into the garden. She blamed her softly, "Why did you wait till today to come? I miss you so much." Feng Sanniang said, "I miss you too. But I am a poor girl, and you are the daughter of a rich family. If I have contact with you, those who cause trouble with false stories will spread embroidered rumors and malicious gossip, making you feel awful." Fan Shiyiniang still did not let her leave. After that, the two girls became as inseparable as body and shadow, and as dear to each other as sisters.

Strange Tales from the Make-Do Studio

飛將數奇

fēi jiāng shǔ qí

飛將軍氣數不好；形容有才能的人命運不佳，遭遇不好。

西漢名將李廣，善騎射，一生與匈奴作戰大小七十餘次，屢建奇功。他任右北平太守時，匈奴被李廣打怕了，數年間不敢犯境，稱他為‘飛將軍’。李廣六十多歲時隨大將軍衛青攻打匈奴，因受到排擠和挫折，遂自殺而死。李廣一生，雖戰績彪炳，卻從未以功封邑。《史記》記載説："李廣……邊郡屢守，大軍再從。失道見斥，數奇不封。惜哉名將，天下無雙！"

出自《史記》

The Winged General Has a Bad Fortune

Said of talented people who have bad fate and bitter experiences.

Li Guang, a famous general of the Western Han Dynasty, was good at horsemanship and archery, had fought over seventy battles against the Xiongnu tribe, and had distinguished himself time and again. While he was magistrate of Beiping Prefecture, Li Guang often defeated the Xiongnu, who called him "Winged General" and dared not harass the border areas for several years. On one occasion, Li Guang, then in his sixties, followed the Grand Marshal Wei Qing to attack the Xiongnu, but later committed suicide becauase this time he suffered setbacks. Though Li Guang had achieved remarkable military exploits throughout his life, he had never been awarded a fief. According to the *Records of the Historian*, "Li Guang...defended the frontier prefecture for many years and became commanding general many times. Reproached for his failures, and having a bad fortune, he had never been granted a noble title. What a pity for the peerless general!"

Records of the Historian

羿射九日

yì shè jiǔ rì

羿射下九個太陽；比喻為民除害、救災解難。

傳説在堯的時候，天上有十個太陽，曬枯了莊稼和所有植物。還有各種兇猛怪獸：叫聲像嬰兒啼哭一樣的猰貐；身長三尺多，有鑿子牙的鑿；長著九顆頭、能噴水吐火的九嬰；力大無比、能興風起浪的大鳥；封豨是兇惡的大野豬；修蛇是巨大的蟒蛇，能把大象吞掉。當時，老百姓的生命受到很大的威脅。堯就派羿帶著弓箭刀槍，射殺十個太陽和各種怪獸。經過殊死博鬥，最後，羿彎弓射下了九個太陽，留一個在天上。

老百姓的災難消除了，生命威脅解除了，萬眾歡騰。羿成為英雄，堯就更受人們愛戴擁護了。

出自《淮南子》

Yi Shoots Down Nine Suns

Said of protecting the people and providing disaster relief.

According to legend, there were ten suns at the time of Yao, drying the crops and plants. There were also ferocious animals: *yayu*, crying like infants; *zao*, with a height of over one meter; *jiuying*, with nine heads, spouting water and fire; giant birds with great strength, raising the wind and waves; *fengxi*, a kind of violent wild boar; and *xiushe*, a huge boa that could devour an elephant. The lives of common people were greatly threatened at that time. Yao sent Yi to shoot the ten suns and animals, and he brought arrows, a bow, knife, and spear with him. Fighting a last-ditch battle, Yi shot down nine suns at last, and left only one in the sky.

The threat to the common people was eliminated, and the threat to their lives removed. The people danced for joy. Yi became a hero, and Yao was admired and supported by everyone.

The Book of Huai Nan Zi

羿射九日

韋編三絕

wéi biān sān jué

編聯竹簡的皮繩斷了多次；形容刻苦好學，勤奮讀書。

孔子是春秋時期傑出思想家和教育家，是儒家的始創者。他有弟子三千人，精通六藝者七十二人。他的主要言行由弟子記載下來，編成《論語》一書，計有二十篇。他也刪改史書，曾改訂魯國史官所編的《春秋》。孔子晚年時，很喜愛讀《周易》，翻來覆去地研讀，竟然使編聯竹簡的牛皮繩斷了好幾次。

出自《史記》

The Bookbinding Snaps Three Times

Said of one who is studious and hardworking.

The Renowned thinker and educator Confucius flourished during the Spring and Autumn Period. He had three thousand pupils, seventy-two of whom were proficient in the Six Arts. Most of his words and deeds were recorded by his pupils, and compiled into the twenty-chapter *Confucian Analects*. He also revised history books, and rewrote the *Spring and Autumn Annals* compiled by historians of the Lu State. Confucius liked reading *The Book of Changes*. In his later years he spent so much time reading it that its leather rope bindings broke many times.

Records of the Historian

畏影惡跡

wèi yǐng wù jī

害怕自己的影子，厭惡自己的足跡；比喻不必要的顧慮。

從前，有一個人，既懼怕自己的身影，又憎嫌自己的足跡。他為了驅開足跡和影子，便來回走著，可這麼一來，足跡反而更多了；他要遠離影子，便急步而行，可是影不離身。他以為自己走得太慢，給影子追上了，便沒命狂奔亂跑，結果疲累而死。

這個愚蠢的人，不曉得只要站在陰暗處，就沒有影子；只要停止不動，就沒有足跡。

出自《莊子》

Scared of His Own Shadow, and Detesting His Own Footprints

Said of unnecessary worries.

Once upon a time, there was a man who was scared of his own shadow and detested his own footprints. In order to get rid of the footprints and shadow he walked back and forth, but his footprinits only increased; he walked fast to leave his shadow behind, but it followed him. He thought he still walked too slowly, allowing the shadow to keep up with him, so he ran about wildly till he was dead tired.

The foolish man did not realize that there would be no shadow if he stood in the dark; there would be no footprints if he stopped moving.

The Book of Zhuang Zi

旁若無人

páng ruò wú rén

旁邊好像沒有人一樣；形容神態自若，目中無人。

荊軻是戰國末的衛國人，喜好讀書擊劍。秦國滅亡衛國後，荊軻逃亡到燕國，燕人稱他為荊卿。荊軻喜歡結交屠狗輩人，後來與高漸離成了好朋友，每天都聚集在街上喝酒。飲至酒興正濃的時候，高漸離擊築，荊軻高聲和唱，兩人有時相對大笑，有時相對哭泣，旁若無人，毫無顧忌。

出自《史記》

Acting As If There Were No One Near

Said of persons who look perfectly calm, and care for nobody.

Jing Ke, of the Wei people, lived at the end of the Warring States Period. After the Qin State destroyed the Wei State, Jing Ke fled to the Yan State, and was called Jing Qing (Sir Jing) by the Yan people. Jing Ke liked to make friends with people of low social status and he became a good friend of Gao Jianli, and they gathered on the street to drink wine every day. When they were in a high mood while drinking wine, Gao Jianli would play a musical instrument called *zhu* and Jing Ke would sing in a high voice. They sometimes laughed loudly, and sometimes cried, face to face, as if there were no one else around, and they had not a worry in the world.

Records of the Historian

剖腹藏珠

pōu fù cǎng zhū

剖開肚子把珍珠藏進去；比喻為了惜物而傷身。

唐太宗李世民，是唐初的傑出皇帝。有一天，他頗有用意地對侍臣們說：“我聽說西域有一個商人得到了一顆明珠，世間少有，他非常珍惜。商人害怕丟失了寶貝，竟然剖開肚皮把珍珠藏了進去。你們說有這樣的事嗎？”侍臣們都說“有”。李世民接著說：“是的，有些官吏因貪贓受賄而喪命，有些皇帝因追求享樂，窮奢極侈而亡國。這不正如西域商人一樣，因惜物而傷身嗎？”

出自《資治通鑒》

Cutting One's Belly Open to Hide a Pearl

Said of harming one's health out of covetousness.

Taizong (Li Shimin) was an outstanding emperor in the early Tang Dynasty. One day, he said to his attendants, "It is said that a businessman in the Western Regions had a rare pearl and treasured it very much. For fear of losing it, he even cut his belly open to hide the pearl. Do you think this is true?" The attendants all said "Yes." Li Shimin continued, saying, "Some government officials lost their lives for accepting bribes, and some emperors caused their states to perish while seeking pleasure and squandering recklessly. Aren't they the same as that businessman who harmed himself for the sake of the pearl?"

History As a Mirror

唐突西施

táng tū xī shī

冒犯了西施；比喻抬高了醜的，貶低了美的。

周顗是晉代的將領，少年時善於談論，很有名望。有一天，他的好友庾亮對他說："現在很多人常常把你比作樂廣了。"樂廣是晉代一位賢人，有著高貴的品德。周顗自覺不能與樂廣相比，誠懇地說："人們將我比作樂廣，這是在畫戰國時的醜女無鹽來和春秋時的美女西施相比，貶低了西施的美啊！"

出自《世說新語》

Offending Xi Shi the Beauty

Said of playing down the beautiful in order to make the ugly more conspicuous.

Zhou Yi was a general of the Jin Dynasty. He was known for his eloquence when he was young. One day, his good friend Yu Liang said to him, "Now many people compare you to Yue Guang." Yue Guang was a person of renowned virtue. Zhou Yi felt that he was not as good as Yue Guang, and said sincerely, "Comparing me to Yue Guang is tantamount to comparing the ugly girl Wu Yan in the Warring States Period with the beauty Xi Shi during the Spring and Autumn Period. It only plays down Xi Shi the beauty!"

New Social Anecdotes

狼狽為奸

láng bèi wéi jiān

比喻壞人合夥幹壞事。

傳說狽是一種前腿很短的走獸，行動時要趴在狼的身上才能走路。狼是一種耳朵直立，尾巴下垂，性情兇殘的野獸。狼和狽勾結起來，狼用前腿，狽用後腿，相互配合行動，伺機傷害牲畜。

出自《酉陽雜俎》

Wolf and Bei Jackal in Cahoots with Each Other

Said of bad people conspiring together to do evil.

Legend has it that *bei* was a jackal-like animal with short forelegs, and has to lie on a wolf's back while walking. The wolf is a violent animal with erect ears and a drooping tail. The wolf and the *bei* cooperate with each other: the wolf walks with his forelegs, and the *bei* with hind legs, they take concerted action, and watch for their chance to attack other animals.

Miscellany of the Youyang Mountains

徒有虛名

tú yǒu xū míng

徒然空有名望；比喻只有虛名，沒有真才實學的人，也形容名不符實的事物。

三國時，諸葛亮率兵北伐魏國，屯兵祁山。忽然接到探子回報：魏國司馬懿率領大軍望祁山殺來。諸葛亮擔憂地說："司馬懿必先奪取街亭，斷我糧道。街亭雖然是小地方，卻是咽喉要地，一旦失守，必誤大事。"蜀將馬謖才氣逼人，善論軍事，向來受諸葛亮器重。他主動請戰，領取精兵防守街亭。

司馬懿派人打聽誰人引兵守街亭。探子回報：防守街亭的將領是馬良的弟弟馬謖。司馬懿聽後，大笑說："馬謖徒有虛名，其實是庸才！"

果然不出司馬懿所料，馬謖不聽王平的勸諫，堅持在山上紮寨，被魏將張部重重圍困，斷絕了水道，跟著放火燒山，蜀兵軍心大亂，四處竄逃，馬謖終於丟失了街亭。

出自《三國演義》

徒有虛名

Existing in Name Only

Said of people who enjoy a reputation unwarranted by any real learning, or of things whose reputations fall far short of the reality.

During the Three Kingdoms Period, Zhuge Liang of the Shu Kingdom led his troops on a punitive expedition north to the Wei State, and stationed them in the Qishan Mountains. Suddenly a scout reported that Sima Yi, a Wei general, was leading his troops toward the Qishan Mountains. Zhuge Liang said anxiously, "Sima Yi will seize Jieting first to cut off our supply line. Though it is a small place, Jieting is a key junction. It would harm matters greatly if Jieting is lost." Ma Su, a general highly regarded by Zhuge Liang, offered to lead picked troops to defend Jieting.

Sima Yi sent a scout off to discover who was leading the enemy troops to defend Jieting. When the scout reported that it was Ma Su, Ma Liang's brother, Sima Yi laughed loudly and said, "Ma Su enjoys undeserved fame, but he is actually a mediocre person!" Things soon developed as Sima Yi expected. Not listening to Wang Ping's advice, Ma Su insisted on encamping on a mountain, and was besieged and encircled by the troops led by the Wei general Zhang He. The Wei troops then began to attack with fire. The water supply being cut off, the morale of the Shu troops began to slump, and the soldiers fled pell-mell. Ma Su finally lost Jieting.

Tales of the Three Kingdoms

乘風破浪

chéng fēng pò làng

乘著風勢，破浪前進；比喻有遠大的抱負，不畏艱難，奮勇前進。

南北朝時，有一個叫宗慤的人，年少時便有雄心壯志。有一天，叔父宗炳和他談到將來的志向時，宗慤豪氣地說："願乘長風，破萬里浪。"宗炳聽後，對他勉勵不已。

後來，宗慤幾經奮鬥，在平定劉劭、劉誕之亂時，立下了戰功，終於成為南北朝時期的名將。

出自《晉書》

乘風破浪

Riding the Wind and Breaking the Waves

Said of people with lofty ideals who are fearless and advance courageously.

During the Southern and Northern Dynasties, there was a man named Zong Que who had great ambitions when he was young. One day, while talking about his aspirations with his uncle Zong Bing, Zong Que said with pride, "I wish to ride the strong wind, and break a thousand waves." Zong Bing praised him for his lofty ideals.

Later in life, Zong Que rendered meritorious services by pacifying the disturbances created by Liu Shao and Liu Dan, and became a famous general of the time.

History of the Jin Dynasty

乘興而來

chéng xìng ér lái

趁著一時的興致而來；泛指高高興興地來。

晉代名士王徽之，曾經在浙江山陰居住。有一年的冬天夜裡，下了一場大雪。他興致很高，一邊賞雪，一邊飲酒。忽然間，想起了住在剡地的好朋友戴安道，他即便連夜乘小船前往探訪。小船在水影銀光中前進，經過一夜，到了剡地。但王徽之卻過門而不入，人家覺得詫異。他說："我本是乘興而來，興盡而返，何必一定要見戴安道呢？"

出自《世說新語》

Coming While in a Joyful Mood

Said of someone coming to a certain place in high spirits, or doing something on an impulse.

Wang Huizhi was a famous man of letters during the Jin Dynasty who lived at Shanyin in present-day Zhejiang Province. One winter night, it snowed heavily. Wang was in high spirits, appreciating the snow while drinking wine. Suddenly, he thought of his good friend Dai Andao who lived in Shan, so he went to visit him by boat that very night. The small boat advanced through the silver light of the waves, and finally reached Shan. However, Wang Huizhi passed his friend's house without entering it. When asked why he did not do so, he said, "I went while in a joyful mood, and returned after having enjoyed myself. Why should I see Dai Andao?"

New Social Anecdotes

捉刀人

zhuō dāo rén

執著刀的人；比喻替人出力或代筆作文章的人。

三國時，魏王（曹操）將要接見匈奴使者，他覺得自已容貌醜陋，不足以顯揚國運。於是，曹操便要崔珪代替他接見匈奴使者，自己裝扮成衛士，執著刀站在坐榻旁邊。

事後，曹操派間諜問匈奴使者："你覺得魏王如何？"使者回答說："魏王雅望非常，但執刀的人，是個英雄啊！"

曹操聽間諜匯報後，馬上派人追殺了使者。

出自《世說新語》

The Man Holding a Sword

Said of people who act or write articles for others.

One day during the Three Kingdoms Period, when Cao Cao, ruler of the Wei Kingdom, was about to meet the Xiongnu envoy, he felt that he was too ugly to represent the state's strength. So Cao Cao asked Cui Gui to meet the envoy instead, while Cao Cao stood by dressed as a bodyguard and holding a sword.

Later, Cao Cao sent a spy to ask the Xiongnu envoy, "How do you feel about the king of Wei?" The envoy answered, "The king of Wei has an extraordinary mien of elegance, while the man holding the sword is a hero!"

Hearing this report from the spy, Cao Cao immediately dispatched someone to kill the envoy.

New Social Anecdotes

氣殺鍾馗

qì shā zhōng kuí

氣死鍾馗；比喻面色難看，滿面怒容。

據説，鍾馗未成為打鬼、驅邪的神以前，本來是唐朝的秀才。有一年，他考中了狀元，但皇帝嫌他的容貌醜陋，打算另外選人。鍾馗氣殺得暴跳如雷，撞柱自刎而死。

出自《鍾馗捉鬼傳》

Zhong Kui Dies of Indignation

Said of people whose face is discolored with anger.

It is said that Zhong Kui was a *xiucai* (scholar who passed the civil examination at the county level) in the Tang Dynasty before he became the Ghost-Taming Deity. One year, he came first in the national civil examination and won the *zhuangyuan* (Number One Scholar). The emperor disliked him, however, because he was ugly, and was about to select another person. Zhong Kui felt so indignant that he stamped with fury, knocking his head on a post and killing himself.

A Tale of Zhong Kui Catching Ghosts

氣殺鍾馗

烏合之眾

wū hé zhī zhòng

像烏鴉一樣暫時湊合；比喻臨時湊合起來的人群。

東漢名將耿弇，在二十一歲那年，王莽的新王朝剛剛失敗，耿弇便率領兵馬投奔漢光武帝劉秀。在行軍途中，部下孫倉、衛包勸耿弇不如投奔王郎。王郎本是以卜相為業，在邯鄲起兵時，冒稱為漢成帝之子劉子輿。耿弇聽後，按劍怒説："我現在到長安領取漁陽、上谷兵馬，再進出太原、代郡，往返只不過數十天，到時回過來收拾王郎這些烏合之眾，就有如摧毀枯枝腐木一樣。"孫、衛二人不理會耿弇，投奔了王郎。

後來，劉秀率兵攻破邯鄲，殺了王郎，而耿弇被封為建威大將軍。

出自《後漢書》

A Crowd Assembling Like Crows

Said of a group of people hastily gathered together for a given task or purpose.

General Geng Yan was only twenty-one years old when he led his troops and went over to Liu Xiu, Emperor Guangwu of the Eastern Han Dynasty, for refuge after Wang Mang's new dynasty failed. Along the march, his subordinates Sun Cang and Wei Bao tried to persuade Geng Yan to join Wang Lang. Wang Lang was originally a sorcerer practicing divination for a living, and when he first rose in revolt at Handan he pretended to be Liu Ziyu, son of Emperor Chengdi of the

Western Han Dynasty. Geng Yan said indignantly, grasping his sword, "I will go to Chang'an to gather the troops of Yuyang and Shanggu, and then go to Taiyuan and Daijun, which takes little more than a month. Then I will return to settle with Wang Lang and his hastily assembled crowds and destroy them like withered branches and rotten trees." Sun and Wei paid no attention to Geng Yan, and went over to Wang Lang.

After that, Liu Xiu led his troops to capture Handan, and killed Wang Lang. Geng Yan was then granted the title of Great Mighty General.

History of the Later Han Dynasty

流連忘返

liú lián wàng fǎn

沉迷遊樂而忘了回去；現在形容對美好景物的留戀。

戰國時，孟子給齊宣王講了一個齊景公巡遊的故事：有一天，齊景公問晏子："君王應如何巡遊？"晏子説："以前的賢君巡遊不是為了遊玩享樂，而是為了體察民情，為治理國家的。現在可不一樣了，君王一旦出遊，必定勞師動眾，所到之處，搜刮民間錢糧，老百姓無不連聲咒罵。這是'流連荒亡'，就是説從上游向下游玩樂而忘返謂之流，從下游到上游玩樂而忘返謂之連，無休止地狩獵謂之荒，不知節制地飲酒作樂謂之亡。過去的賢君都不會'流連荒亡'。"齊宣王聽了這個故事後，似乎若有所思。

出自《孟子》

So Lost in Enjoyment As to Forget to Go Home

Said of people so enchanted by beautiful scenery as to forget to leave for home.

During the Warring States Period, Mencius told King Xuan of the Qi State a story about Duke Jing of Qi's inspection tour. One day, Duke Jing asked Yan Zi, "How should a ruler undertake an inspection tour?" Yan Zi said, "Virtuous sovereigns in the past took tours not for enjoyment and pleasure, but to observe the people's conditions for better administration of his state. But things are different nowadays. Once a ruler goes on a tour, he mobilizes too many troops and people, and extorts money and food from the people wherever he goes, so the ordinary people all curse repeatedly. This is called '*liu lian huang wang*': *liu* means to go sightseeing from the upper reaches to the lower reaches of a river, and forget to return; *lian* means to go sightseeing from the lower reaches to the upper reaches of a river, and forget to return; *huang* means to hunt ceaselessly, and *wang* means to drink wine and seek pleasure without restraint. None of the virtuous rulers in the past did these things." Hearing this story, King Xuan became absorbed in thought.

The Book of Mencius

莫須有

mò xū yǒu

恐怕有，也許有；後用來形容憑空揑造罪名，陷害別人。

南宋紹興九年，宰相秦檜力主向金國投降稱臣，抗金名將岳飛屢次上表反對。第二年，金國進兵河南，岳飛率領‘岳家軍’大破金兵主力，接著，再揮軍朱仙鎮，收復了鄭州、洛陽等地。這時，秦檜求和心切，唆擺宋高宗一日連降十二道金牌召岳飛回師。岳飛回臨安後，不僅被解除了兵權。不久還被誣下獄。

名將韓世忠怒憤填膺，當面斥責秦檜，要秦檜拿出真憑實據來證實岳飛、岳雲父子謀反。秦檜說："岳飛與張憲在信上雖沒有說謀反的事，但事體莫須有。"韓世忠悲憤地說："莫須有三字何以服天下！？"

紹興十一年十二月二十九日，'莫須有'三字，害了一代名將的性命。

出自《宋史》

莫須有

It Might Be True

Said of making a false charge against someone by fabricating an accusation.

In the ninth year of the Shaoxing reign in the Southern Song Dynasty, the Prime Minister Qin Hui strongly advocated surrendering to the Jin State. The famous general Yue Fei advised the emperor against this many times. The Jin troops marched toward Henan the following year. Yue Fei led his army to defeat the main force of the Jin troops, then ordered his men to advance on the town of Zhuxian, and also recovered Zhengzhou, Luoyang, and other cities. At this moment, eager to sue for peace, Qin Hui persuaded Emperor Gaozong to summon Yue Fei to lead his troops back by continuously sending out twelve orders. After Yue Fei returned to Linan (now Hangzhou), his military leadership was revoked and he was framed and put into prison.

Filled with indignation, the famous general Han Shizhong accused Qin Hui to his face and asked him to produce conclusive evidence to prove that Yue Fei and his son Yue Yun had plotted a rebellion. Qin Hui said, "Though Yue Fei and his subordinate general Zhang Xian did not talk about rebellion in their letters, it might be true." Han Shizhong said with grief and indigantion, "How can you convince people with the words 'it might be true'?" On the twenty-ninth day of the twelfth lunar month in the eleventh year of the Shaoxing reign, the phrase "it might be true" brought death to the famous general.

History of the Song Dynasty

莫蹪於山，而蹪於垤

mò tuí yú shān, ér tuí yú dié

沒有被山絆倒，卻被小土堆絆倒了；比喻小事易被忽視，以致造成了錯誤。

淮南王劉安是漢高祖的孫子，好讀書鼓琴，好求神仙之道，善於文辭。曾受漢武帝重視，後來因謀反事而自殺。但由劉安招攬數千人撰寫的《淮南鴻烈》，又叫《淮南子》的著作卻流傳後世。

《淮南子》在論述人間之事時說："人們都沒有被大山絆倒，反而會被小土堆絆倒了。這是由於人們往往輕視了小問題、小事情，以致造成了錯誤，才覺得後悔。"

出自《淮南子》

Stumbled by a Mound Instead of a Mountain

Said of making mistakes because of overlooking small things.

Liu An, also known as Prince Huainan, grandson of Emperor Gaozu of the Han Dynasty, enjoyed reading, playing musical instruments, and seeking divine advice, and had excellent diction. Emperor Wudi thought highly of him, but he committed suicide after plotting a rebellion. However, the *Hero Prince Huainan*, also called *The Book of Huai Nan Zi*, written by thousands of people recruited by Liu An, was handed down to later generations.

It was said in *The Book of Huai Nan Zi*: "People stumble over mounds instead of great mountains, because they often overlook small problems and things, which leads to mistakes, and then they live to regret it."

The Book of Huai Nan Zi

剛愎自用

gāng bì zì yòng

固執而自以為是；形容非常固執自信，不聽別人的意見。

有一年，鄭國被楚軍圍困了三個月，終於被逼投降，與楚國結了盟。這時，趕來救援鄭國的晉國荀林父聽說鄭國已經與楚國結盟，便說："鄭、楚已經講和，等楚軍退走後，再與鄭國算賬吧。"副手先縠不同意說："晉國的軍隊就是因為英勇作戰，才雄霸諸侯。哪有碰到楚軍就逃跑？你們即管退縮，我可不幹！"先縠率領部份兵馬，攻打楚軍去了。

楚國大臣伍參聽說先縠來攻，對楚莊王說："荀林父新任中軍之帥，初掌國事，政令不通。尤其是先縠，剛愎不仁，固執抗命。晉國軍將不睦，有令不行，晉軍必敗無疑。"

出自《左傳》

Headstrong and Opinionated

Said of being obstinate and overconfident.

Once when it was being besieged by the Chu troops for three months, the Zheng State was forced to surrender, and aligned itself with Chu. Hearing that Zheng had aligned with Chu, General Xun Linfu of the Jin State, who had been ordered to come to rescue Zheng, said, "Zheng and Chu have made peace with each other, so we had better settle accounts with Zheng after the Chu troops withdraw." The aide Xian Hu disagreed with him, "The Jin troops dominated the other states beacause of their bravery in battle. Why should we flee when meeting the Chu troops? You may shrink back, but I won't!" Xian Hu then led soldiers to attack the Chu troops.

Learning that Xian Hu was coming to attack them, Wu Can, a minister of Chu, said to King Zhuang, "Xun Linfu was newly appointed the commanding general. He has no understanding of government decrees because he just wields power. Xian Hu is especially stubborn and unkind, and disobeys orders. The Jin general and his assistant are not in harmony, and the assistant disobeys order, so the Jin troops will surely fail."

Zuo Qiuming's Chronicles

殺彘教子

shā zhì jiào zǐ

比喻父母以身作則，說話算數，教子誠實無欺。

春秋時的一天，曾參的妻子要到集市去，兒子又哭又鬧地跟在身後。曾參的妻子哄他說："乖孩子，別哭，你先回家去，等我回來殺豬給你吃。"曾參的妻子回來後，看見曾參正要殺豬，慌忙去阻攔，說："我只不過是騙騙孩子的啊！"曾參說："孩子是天真無邪的，很自然要向父母學習的。如今你欺騙兒子，等於教兒子欺騙別人；母親欺騙兒子，兒子也就不相信母親，這不是好的家教呀！"曾參堅持殺豬給孩子吃，以表示父母的言行一致。

出自《韓非子》

Killing the Pig to Teach the Child

Said of parents setting an example to teach their children honesty.

One day during the Spring and Autumn Period, Zeng Shen's wife was about to go to the market, and their son followed her, making a tearful scene. The wife tried to trick the boy, saying, "Don't cry, there's a good child. Go home now, and I will kill a pig for you to eat after I come back." When the wife returned to find that Zeng Shen was about to kill the pig, she tried to stop him, "I only wanted to coax the baby!" Zeng Shen said, "Children are innocent, and they will naturally learn from their parents. In trying to cheat our son, you will teach him to fool others; if a mother cheats her son, the son will not believe his mother. This is not good family education!" Zeng Shen insisted on killing the pig for the child to eat to show that his parents match their words with their deeds.

The Book of Han Fei Zi

卿卿我我

qīng qīng wǒ wǒ

'卿卿' 是男女間的互稱、愛稱；形容夫妻、男女間的親密關係。

據説，王安豐的夫人平日喜歡親密地稱呼夫君。有一天，王安豐對夫人說："你整天那麼親密的叫我，這是對禮法的不敬，以後可別這樣了。"夫人親昵地說："親卿、愛卿，是以卿卿，我不卿卿，誰當卿卿？"此後，王安豐的夫人還是'卿卿'不息。

出自《世説新語》

Qing-Qing-Wo-Wo

Terms of endearment between lovers. Also refering to intimate relations between couples.

It is said that Wang Anfeng's wife liked to speak to her husband in intimate ways. One day, Wang Anfeng said to his wife, "You always call me pet names, which is not respectful of the code of rites. Please stop doing it." The wife said, very intimately, "*Qing qing, ai qing, shi yi qing qing, wo bu qing qing, shui dang qing qing*?" ("Honey, my dear love, my loved one, who may call you by these terms but me?") After that, Wang Anfeng's wife continued to use these peculiar endearing terms of hers while addressing her husband.

New Social Anecdotes

魚目混珠

yú mù hùn zhū

魚眼珠冒充珍珠；比喻以假亂真。

從前，有一個叫滿願的人，買了一顆又圓又大、光彩奪目的珍珠。他很珍重地收藏起來。滿願的鄰居壽量，有一天在路上拾到一顆又圓又大的魚眼珠，他以為是顆珍珠，也很小心地收藏起來。

後來，有人患了病，需要用珍珠配藥才能治好，便出高價到處收購珍珠。滿願知道後，把珍珠拿出來，壽量也把魚眼珠拿出來。兩顆珠子放在一起，立刻就分辨出真假了。這正是："魚目豈為珠，蓬蒿不成櫃。（野草不能冒充茶樹）"

出自《參同契》

魚目混珠

Passing Off Fish Eyes As Pearls

Said of passing off something fake as genuine.

Long, long ago, a man named Man Yuan bought a big, round, brilliant pearl and carefully stored it. His neighbor Shou Liang picked up a big, round fish eye one day and considered it a pearl and also stored it carefully.

Later on, when a person who was ill needed a pearl for medicine, Man Yuan and Shou Liang took out their pearl and fish eye together. It was easy to distinguish which was the pearl and the patient said, "How can a fish eye be a pearl? Wild grass can't be passed off as tea."

Combining Three Taoist Principles in One

假途滅虢

jiǎ tú miè guó

借別國的路，消滅了虢國；形容先借人家的路，回途時順便連借路人也吞掉。

春秋時的晉國向虞國借路征伐虢國，虞公不聽下屬的勸告，答允了晉國的要求。晉國消滅了虢國，回師途中順便滅了虞國。

出自《左傳》

Borrowing a Road to Conquer the State of Guo

Said of first conquering one state by passing through another state's territory and then turning back to conquer the other state.

In the Spring and Autumn Period, the state of Jin asked the state of Yu for the right to use its road to invade the state of Guo. The ruler of Yu permitted this without heeding the advice of his ministers. The Jin troops then destroyed the state of Guo, and then the state of Yu on their way home.

Zuo Qiuming's Chronicles

黃袍加身

huàng páo jiā shēn

皇帝的袍服加在身上；比喻受部屬的擁護而當了皇帝；也比

喻靠陰謀而取得成功。

後周時，趙匡胤任殿前都點檢，奉命領軍抵禦契丹的入侵。公元九六〇年，在一天夜裡五更時分，部下將領齊集在驛門，宣佈擁立趙匡胤為王，趙匡胤裝作制止不及，被部屬們把皇帝穿的黃袍披在身上，擁立為帝，建立了宋王朝。

出自《宋史》

Draped with the Imperial Yellow Robe

Said of being acclaimed emperor or making one's mark by underhand methods.

During the Late Zhou Dynasty, Zhao Kuangyin, the inspector-general at court, was ordered to resist Qidan. In the year 960 his subordinates declared him emperor. Zhao Kuangyin pretended to stop them, but was draped with the imperial yellow robe by his supporters, and hence established the Song Dynasty.

History of the Song Dynasty

萬死不辭

wàn sǐ bù cí

儘管要死一萬次，也不會推辭；形容願意竭誠效勞的決心。

東漢末年，董卓專斷了朝政。大臣王允很為漢室的江山而擔憂。一天夜裡，王允心裡煩悶，到後花園散心。忽然聽見有人在嘆氣，王允聽清楚，原來是家中的歌伎貂蟬。王允問她是怎麼一回事，貂蟬說："我受大人養育之恩，又教我熟習歌舞，一直以禮相待。我粉身碎骨，也難報大人恩惠的萬一。近日見大人兩眉深鎖，必定有難以解決的國家大事，又不敢問大人。今晚又為此而坐立不安，長嗟短嘆，想不到給大人碰見了。大人如用得著我，萬死不辭！"

王允於是利用貂蟬的美色，施用'連環計'。先把貂蟬許配給董卓的義子呂布，然後暗中獻給董卓，離間了他們父子感情。後來，呂布終於把董卓殺了。

出自《三國演義》

Not To Be Daunted by Ten Thousand Deaths

Said of determination to fulfill a task.

During the later years of the Eastern Han Dynasty, when Dong Zhuo arrogated all powers to himself, Minister Wang Yun worried about the future of the dynasty. One evening, Wang Yun was pondering this while walking in the garden. Suddenly, he heard somebody sigh. It was his family singing-girl Diao Chan. Wang Yun asked her what was happening and Diao Chan said, "You brought me up and taught me to sing and dance and treated me with respect. I can not repay your kindness enough, even by dying the most cruel death. I find you deeply worried these days; it must be over some difficult national affair. But I dare not ask you, so I am fidgety tonight and sighing. If you need my help, I will not flinch from it even if I will have to die ten thousand times for it!"

Wang Yun then made a set of interlocking stratagems by using the beauty of Diao Chan. First, he let Diao Chan engage to be married to Dong Zhuo's adopted son Lu Bu, and then presented Diao Chan to Dong Zhuo secretly in order to sow discord between them. After this, Lu Bu killed Dong Zhuo.

Tales of the Three Kingdoms

萬里長城

wàn lǐ cháng chéng

比喻足以依靠的堅強力量；也比喻國家賴以守衛疆土的將領或軍隊。

南朝宋名將檀道濟，因為屢建奇功，以致威名太盛，功高震主，為梁文帝所忌。梁文帝一意要殺害他。當檀道濟被朝廷逮捕時，憤怒氣極，目光如炬，頃刻間喝了杯酒，把頭巾摜在地上說："這是毀壞了國家的萬里長城！"

出自《南史》

萬里長城

The Great Wall

Said of steadfast power, or the generals and troops protecting the country's border.

As a famous general of the state of Song of the Southern Dynasties, Tan Daoji rendered many meritorious services which made his reputation higher than that of Emperor Wendi of Liang, and the emperor wanted to kill him. When Tan Daoji was arrested at court, he was extremely angry, his eyes blazing like torches. He drank a glass of wine and threw his kerchief down on the ground, saying, "This is to destroy the Great Wall of the country!"

History of the Southern Dynasties

捨命陪君子

shě mìng péi jūn zǐ

豁出性命，奉陪您盡興到底。

明朝正德年間，李西涯任翰林時，有一天陪郡侯飲酒。兩人飲過了頭，李西涯醉昏昏地說："屬下今日捨命陪君子了。"郡侯樂呵呵說："晚輩也不是君子，老先生不要輕生呀。"

出自《古今譚概》

I Would Throw My Lot in with You, Sir, at the Risk of My Life

Said of jocularly agreeing to join someone.

During the Zhengde reign of the Ming Dynasty, one day Li Xiya, an academician of the Imperial Academy, was drinking with a prefecture magistrate, and they all had too much to drink. Li Xiya said tipsily, "Today I would throw my lot in with you, sir, at the risk of my life." The prefecture magistrate smiled, "I'm not a sir, old chap, don't commit suicide."

Anecdotes Past and Present

掃榻以迎

sǎo tà yǐ yíng

清除榻上的灰塵，迎接客人的來臨；形容熱誠地歡迎來客。

東漢大臣陳蕃，不畏強權，極力反對宦官專權。他任豫章太守時，從來不接待來訪的客人。徐稚是一位高士，因為不滿宦官擅權，雖然受多次徵召，始終不為官。當徐稚到訪陳蕃時，陳蕃立即清除榻上的塵垢，迎接他的來臨。

出自《後漢書》

Sweeping the Bed Clean in Expectation of a Visitor

Said of looking forward to a guest's visit.

A senior official of the Eastern Han Dynasty, Chen Fan, had no fear of authority and fought against the court eunuchs who were trying to monopolize power. When he was magistrate of Yuzhang, he never received visitors. Xu Zhi was another man of noble character who refused to be an official despite the emperor's repeated summons, resentful of the eunuchs' attempt to monopolizing power. When Xu Zhi visited Chen Fan, Chen at once swept the bed clean in expectation of his visit.

History of the Later Han Dynasty

割蓆斷交

gē xí duàn jiāo

割開蓆子，斷絕交往；形容朋友間因意見不合而絕交。

三國時，管寧與華歆是好朋友。兩人一同生活，一同在一條蓆子上讀書。有一天，他們在菜園裡幹活，發現了一塊金子。管寧看也不看，華歆馬上把金子拾起來，看了幾眼，才擲到一邊。又有一天，正當兩人坐在蓆子上讀書，剛巧有一位官員的乘車路過門前，管寧不為所動，專心讀書；而華歆立刻把書本扔下，趕緊跑出去看熱鬧了。管寧忍受不了華歆的行為，拿起刀子把坐蓆割開，並說："你不是我的朋友。"

後來，管寧終身不為官，避居遼東三十多年，成為隱士；而華歆也達到願望，當了大官。

出自《世說新語》

Cutting the Mat to Break with an Old Friend

Said of breaking off with one's friend over a difference of opinion.

During the Three Kingdoms Period, Guan Ning and Hua Xin were good friends. They lived together and read together on the same mat. One day, they found a gold ingot while working in the vegetable garden. Guan Ning took no notice of it, while Hua Xin picked it up, took a look, and then threw it away. On another day, while they were reading on the mat, an official passed by in a carriage as Guan Ning continued to read his book; Hua Xin put down his book and rushed right out. Guan Ning could not bear Hua Xin's behavior, so he cut the mat and said, "You are not my friend." Later on, Guan Ning became a hermit in Liaodong for more than thirty years; Hua Xin became a high official, as he always wished.

New Social Anecdotes

終南捷徑

zhōng nán jié jìng

終南山是條捷徑；比喻求取官職、名利的捷徑。

唐朝時的盧藏用一心想入朝做官，於是便假裝為隱士，居住在京城附近的終南山裡，希望引起皇帝的注意。後來，果然被召為官。同時期的司馬承禎也用同樣的方法當了官。一天，盧藏用指著終南山說："這山裡面大有佳處。"司馬承禎說："依我看來，此為仕途之捷徑而矣。"

出自《世說新語》

A Short Cut in Mount Zhongnan

Said of short cuts to high office or fame.

Lu Zangyong of the Tang Dynasty wanted to be an official, so he posed as a recluse living on Mount Zhongnan near the capital city to attract the emperor's attention. Some time later, the emperor actually did ask him to be an official. Sima Chengzhen, a contemporary, used the same method to be an official. One day, Lu Zangyong pointed to Mount Zhongnan and said, "There are many nice sites on the mountain." Sima Chengzhen replied, "In my view, it is a short cut to high office."

New Social Anecdotes

強不知以為知

qiǎng bù zhī yǐ wéi zhī

形容不懂裝懂。

子路是孔子的學生，為人直言勇敢，願意聽取別人的批評意見。但他有時卻喜歡牽強附會，自以為是。所以，孔子教導他說：“自己懂得的就是懂的，自己不懂的，就要老老實實承認不懂；這才是真的懂得道理啊！”

出自《論語》

Making a Pretense of Knowledge

Said of pretending to know when one does not know.

Zi Lu, a pupil of Confucius, was brave and frank and often wished to listen to criticism by others. But sometimes he liked to draw forced analogies and was opinionated. So, Confucius said to him, "Say it if you know something, but never pretend if you don't know something; doing so proves you really know the truth!"

Confucian Analects

善自為謀

shàn zì wéi móu

善於謀劃，也形容善於為自己打算。

王僧虔是南齊時著名的書法家，他繼承了王羲之的家傳祖法，善工正、行書。有一天，南齊太祖要和他比賽書法。太祖是個能文、善寫草書的皇帝。兩人寫完字後，太祖說："誰為第一？"王僧虔回答說："我的字第一，陛下亦第一。"太祖笑著說："你真會善自為謀。"

出自《南齊書》

Knowing How to Look After Oneself

Said of someone who is good at taking care of his own interests.

The famous calligrapher of Southern Qi, Wang Zengqian, inherited the skill of his ancestor Wang Xizhi, and excelled at the running hand style. One day, the emperor of Southern Qi, who was good at the cursive script, wanted to compete at calligraphy with him. After finishing his writing, the emperor asked, "Who is number one?" Wang Zengqian replied, "I'm number one and Your Majesty is also number one." The emperor smiled, "You really know how to look after yourself."

History of the Southern Qi Dynasty

超群絕倫

chāo qún jué lún

形容超出很多人，沒有能與其相比、匹敵的。

三國時期，關羽是蜀國的五虎將之一。他英勇善戰，武功超卓，為蜀國立下了許多汗馬功勞，深受劉備的重用。但關羽為人驕傲，器量較淺。

有一次，劉備率軍攻打四川，諸葛亮用計收服了四川守將馬超。關羽知道後，寫信給諸葛亮探問馬超的才能誰人可及。諸葛亮很瞭解他的心情，寫信回答說："馬超文武兼備，勇猛過人，可與漢初的黥、彭二將相比，也可與張飛相提並論。但遠不如你超群絕倫，無人能及。"關羽看完信後，十分高興。

出自《三國志》

超群絕倫

Far Above the Ordinary

Head and Shoulders Above

Said of someone who finds no equals among his peers.

During the Three Kingdoms Period, Guan Yu was one of five famous generals of the Shu Kingdom. He was brave and skillful in battle and had superior military accomplishments, so he had always been put in important positions by Liu Bei. But he was also arrogant and narrow-minded.

Once when Liu Bei attacked Sichuan, Zhuge Liang subdued Sichuan's general Ma Chao by using superior tactics. Guan Yu wrote to Zhuge Liang to ask who could compare with Ma Chao. Zhuge Liang knew well about his feelings and replied, "Ma Chao was well versed in both polite letters and martial arts. His valor and vigor can be compared with the generals of the early Han Dynasty, Qing and Peng, or contemporary Zhang Fei. But you're matchless, nobody can be compared with you." Guan Yu was highly pleased with Zhuge Liang's reply.

History of the Three Kingdoms

雁足傳書

yàn zú chuán shū

比喻傳送書信。

公元前一〇〇年，漢武帝派遣蘇武出使匈奴。匈奴君主單于卻軟硬兼施妄圖逼蘇武投順匈奴。蘇武正氣凜然，寧死不屈。單于沒有辦法，就將蘇武放逐到遙遠而人煙稀少的北海（今貝加爾湖）邊牧羊。蘇武在苦寒的北海捕野鼠、掘野草為食，堅持十九年不降匈奴。

漢昭帝即位的時候，匈奴與漢朝和親。漢昭帝要匈奴放回蘇武。但匈奴使詐，說蘇武早已死去。當漢朝使節再出使匈奴時，從一個叫常惠的匈奴人處獲悉了蘇武仍在北海牧羊的消息並一起擬定了一個計策。第二天，漢朝使者見單于時，就按計策說："漢昭帝在林中打獵，射下了一隻大雁，發現雁腿上繫著一封帛書，原來是蘇武寫的，說他仍在某地的湖澤邊牧羊。"單于聽後，大驚失色，以為蘇武得到神仙幫助，於是將蘇武送回漢朝。

出自《漢書》

Wild Geese Deliver Letters

Said of passing on important messages.

In 100 B.C., Emperor Wudi of the Han Dynasty dispatched Su

Wu to Xiongnu. The chief of the Xiongnu tried by hook or by crook to force Su Wu to surrender, but Su Wu would rather die than submit, and the Xiongnu chief exiled Su Wu to remote, sparsely populated North Sea (today's Lake Baikal) to herd sheep. Su Wu lived there for nineteen years by hunting wild mice and digging wild grass.

When Emperor Zhaodi of the Han Dynasty ascended the throne, relations between Xiongnu and Han became better through marriage. Emperor Zhaodi then asked Xiongnu to return Su Wu. But Xiongnu lied and told Han that Su Wu had died long ago. When an emissary from Han went to Xiongn he heard from a native named Chang Hui that Su Wu was still herding sheep in North Sea, and he devised a plan. Next day, the emissary met the Xiongnu ruler and said, "When Emperor Zhaodi hunted in the forest, he shot a goose and found a letter from Su Wu on its foot. It said he still herds sheep near a lake somewhere." The Xiongnu chief turned pale with fright and thought that Su Wu had gotten help from the immortals, so he sent Su Wu back to the Han Dynasty.

History of the Han Dynasty

虛有其表

xū yǒu qí biǎo

空有好看的外貌；形容外表好看，實際上不行或有名無實。

唐玄宗時，有個叫蕭嵩的人，生得魁梧濃髯，相貌堂堂。有一次，唐玄宗命他起草詔書，唐玄宗看後，很不滿意。蕭嵩退下後，唐玄宗把起草的詔書擲在地上說：“虛有其表罷了。”

出自《明皇雜錄》

Looking Impressive but Lacking Real Worth

Meaning appearances are sometimes deceiving.

At the time of Emperor Xuanzong of the Tang Dynasty, there was a man named Xiao Song who was big and tall and had a thick beard. One day, the emperor ordered him to draft an imperial edict. When this was done, the emperor was dissatisfied with it. After Xiao Song went out, the emperor threw the edict down and said, "He looks impressive, but he lacks real worth."

Random Notes of Emperor Minghhuang

期期艾艾

qī qī āi āi

形容口吃，說話重複不利索；也形容不知措詞而結結巴巴。

有一年，漢高祖打算廢除太子。大臣周昌在朝廷上直言諫止，與劉邦爭論起來。劉邦要他說出道理來。周昌為人口吃，又氣在頭上，說："臣雖然說不出話來，但臣期期知道不能這樣做。陛下要廢太子，臣期期不奉詔。"

三國時，魏國將領鄧艾也是口吃的人，說到自已的時候，連說'艾艾'。有一次，晉文王戲弄他說："你說艾艾，到底是幾艾？"鄧艾答道："鳳兮鳳兮，故是一鳳。"

後來，'期期'、'艾艾'連用，形容口吃，說話不利索。

出自《史記》、《世說新語》

Qi-Qi-Ai-Ai

Said of stuttering or not knowing how to speak.

One year, when Emperor Gaozu of the Han Dynasty wanted to de-throne the crown prince, Minister Zhou Chang used blunt words to dissuade the emperor. When Liu Bang asked him to give his reasons Zhou Chang spoke in an angry stutter, "Although I can't speak, I *qi qi* know you should not do that. If Your Majesty wants to *qi qi* de-throne the crown prince, I *qi qi* will not receive your order."

During the Three Kingdoms Period, the general of the Wei Kingdom, Deng Ai, also spoke with a stutter. Whenever he mentioned himself, he always said "*ai ai.*" Once King Wen of the Jin Dynasty made fun of him, "You talked of *ai ai*, how many *ais*?" Deng Ai replied, "Phoenix, phoenix, it is just one phoenix."

So people use "*qi qi ai ai*" to refer to stutterers.

Records of the Historian and New Social Anecdotes

紫氣東來

zǐ qì dōng lái

祥瑞之氣從東而來；比喻吉祥的徵兆。

傳説老子有一次西遊，當他出函谷關時，關令尹見到有紫氣從東面而來，預示著不久將有聖人到來。一會兒，果然是老子騎著青牛過關，關令尹連忙恭敬地接待他，並請他寫下了《道德經》。

出自《列仙傳》

The Purple Air Comes from the East

Said of good omens.

It is said that once when Lao Zi traveled west, as he was coming out of the Hangu Pass the official in charge of the pass saw purple air coming from the east, a sign that a sage would soon arrive. After a while, Lao Zi came by riding a blue ox. The official received him with respect and asked him to write *Tao Te Ching* or *Dao De Jing* (*The Way and Its Virtue* or *The Book of Lao Zi*).

Biographies of Virtuous Women

紫氣東來

極樂世界

jí lè shì jiè

阿彌陀佛居住的國土；後泛指最快樂、最光明、最清淨的地方。

佛教徒認為：在阿彌陀佛成道時依願而建的，遠在西方的地方裡，有超過十萬億的佛士。在這個世界裡的眾生，無一切人間煩惱，無一切人間的陋習，這樣的淨土，叫作‘極樂世界’。

出自《阿彌陀經》

Western Paradise

Said of the place where Amitabha lived originally, a most happy, bright, and pure land.

Buddhists believe that in a far western land built according to the wishes of Amitabha at the time of his attainment of Buddhahood, there are more than a hundred billion Buddhists. People there have no trouble or bad habits like they do in this world. This pure land is called the Western Paradise.

Amitabha Sutra

貽笑大方

yí xiào dà fāng

給見多識廣的人笑話；比喻被內行人譏笑。

秋天，大小河裡的水都漲起來，匯流入黃河，黃河的河面寬闊起來。人們站在岸邊，看不清對岸的牛馬。這時候，黃河之神河伯洋洋自得，以為天下最壯觀的景色為他所有。河伯沿著河道往東走去，一直走到了渤海，他向前一看，渤海浩瀚無邊。

這時，河伯嘆息說：“今天，我才知道海的無窮無盡，如果我不到這裡來看看，就貽笑大方，給那些有見識的人譏笑了。”

出自《莊子》

貽笑大方

Exposing Oneself to Ridicule by the Knowledgeable

Said of being laughed at by experts.

One autumn, all rivers swelled and ran to the Yellow River. The river was so wide that people couldn't see oxen or horses on the opposite bank. The God of the Yellow River, Hebo, was pleased with himself and considered this most splendid scene his own. He walked east along the river until he reached the Bohai Sea. There he found the sea was so vast that it extended to the end of the horizon.

At this moment, Hebo sighed, "Today, I know the sea is endless. If I did not come here, I'd be laughed at by experts for not knowing that the Yellow River is not the widest in the world."

The Book of Zhuang Zi

董狐直筆

dǒng hú zhí bǐ

董狐如實記載；比喻根據史實，不阿權勢的正直史家。

春秋時，趙盾掌握晉國的國政。後來，由於逃避晉靈公殺害，愴惶逃走。他逃出國境前，弟弟趙穿殺了晉靈公。趙盾回來擁立弟弟趙穿為國君。史官董狐認為趙盾是執掌國事的大臣，要負上趙穿弒君的責任。董狐在史策上記載："趙盾弒君。"

孔子稱讚說："董狐是正直的史家，不懼權貴，如實記載。"

出自《左傳》

Dong Hu's Straight Writing Brush

Said of upright historians who wrote history strictly on the basis of facts, not stooping to flattery to the powerful and influential.

In the Spring and Autumn Period, Zhao Dun took power in the state of Jin and later fled the state to avoid being killed by Duke Ling, the ruler of Jin. His brother Zhao Chuan eventually killed Duke Ling and Zhao Dun made his brother the ruler of Jin. The historian Dong Hu thought Zhao Dun as the senior minister should be responsible for the murder of the duke and so wrote, "Zhao Dun was the one who killed the sovereign of the state." Confucius praised him saying, "Dong Hu is an upright historian and never feared powerful people."

Zuo Qiuming's Chronicles

過門不入

guò mén bù rù

經過家門都不進去；形容公而忘私，勤懇工作。

傳說在堯、舜的時代，發生了洪水氾濫。當時是一個叫鯀的人負責治理洪水，可是治了九年還不見成效。到了舜主政的時候，鯀的兒子禹接替了治理洪水的職務。

禹汲取了父親的經驗，採取了疏導的方法，依據山形地勢開鑿水道，將水引入大海。經過十三年的苦幹，終於治理了洪水。

禹在治理洪水的十三年間，吃盡苦頭，雖然有好幾次經過家門，也不敢回家稍事休息，專心為治理洪水而奮鬥。

禹因為治水有功，舜就把領袖的職位讓給了禹。

出自《史記》

Passing One's Own House but Never Going In

Said of one devoted to public service to the neglect of one's personal interests.

It is said that the rivers were in flood in the time of Yao and Shun. A man named Gun was in charge of bringing the flood under control. But no effect was gained in nine years. When Shun headed the administration, Yu, son of Gun, took over his father's post.

Drawing lessons from his father's failures, Yu had some of the rivers dredged and canals cut to divert floodwaters into the sea. After thirteen years of hard work, he at last made the grade.

During all those years, Yu suffered many privations. He passed his house many times, but he never went in.

For Yu's achievement in controlling flood, Shun gave up the throne to Yu.

Records of the Historian

解鈴還須繫鈴人

jiě líng hái xū jì líng rén

比喻誰惹出問題來，仍由誰去解決。

金陵有一個叫法燈的和尚，生性豪邁，不拘小節，對佛法、佛規毫不在意。因而許多和尚都看不起他，唯獨法眼法師對他另眼相看，十分器重他。

有一天，法眼法師出了一個題目考問眾人："有一頭猛虎，脖子上繫了一個金鈴，誰能把金鈴解下來呢？"和尚們面面相覷，誰也回答不了。剛好法燈來到，法眼法師再複述一次題目。法燈隨口就說："誰繫上去的，誰就能解下來。"法眼法師對眾人說："你們還敢輕視他嗎？"

出自《指月錄》

Better Let Him Who Tied the Bell Untie It

Meaning whoever starts trouble should end it.

Once there was a monk named Fa Deng who lived in Jinling. He neglected minor points of conduct and took no notice of Buddhist doctrines. So the other monks looked down on him, but Master Fa Yan thought highly of him.

One day, Master Fa Yan asked this question, "A tiger has a golden bell tied around its neck. Who can untie the bell?" None of the monks could answer the question. Fa Deng happened to come in, and Master Fa Yan asked him the question. Fa Deng replied at once, "The person who tied the bell can untie it." Master Fa Yan then asked the others, "Do you still look down upon him?"

Pointing to the Moon

盡忠報國

jìn zhōng bào guó

盡心竭力，犧牲一切來報效國家。

岳飛是宋朝的名將，自幼習文。十六歲時，正是國家多事之秋。他的父親命他習武，保衛國家。

岳飛二十歲時從軍，但不久父親去世，回鄉奔喪，在家守孝。宋欽宗靖康二年，金兵南下侵宋，擄走徽、欽二帝。岳母命岳飛再次從軍，誓雪靖康之恥。臨走時，岳母含著淚，咬緊牙根用繡花針在岳飛背上正脊之中刺上‘盡忠報國’四個字。

岳飛英勇善戰，運籌帷幄，帶領宋軍打了不少勝仗。使金人折服得驚呼‘撼山易，撼岳家軍難’！

出自《宋史》

盡忠報國

Serving One's Country Loyally

Said of devotion to one's country.

Yue Fei, a famous general during the Song Dynasty, studied polite letters from childhood. When he was sixteen the country was going through troubled times and his father let him learn martial arts to help protect the country.

Yue Fei joined the army at twenty, but not long after that his father died and he returned home to observe the period of mourning. In the second year of the Jingkang period of Emperor Qinzong's reign, Jin troops invaded the Song Dynasty and kidnaped former Emperor Huizong and Emperor Qinzong. Yue Fei's mother let him join the army again to avenge this insult. Before he left, his mother tearfully tattooed "devotion to the country" on his back with an embroidery needle.

Yue Fei was brave and skillful in battle and won many victories. People of the state of Jin were filled with admiration and said, "It's easier to push a mountain away than move the troops under Yue Fei."

History of the Song Dynasty

豎子成名

shù zǐ chéng míng

小子獲得名聲；對別人的成名表示輕蔑和不服氣；也用作自謙之辭。

戰國時的孫臏和龐涓曾在鬼谷子門下一起學習兵法。魏惠王時，任命了龐涓為將軍。龐涓嫉忌孫臏的軍事才能，派人以敘舊的名義騙孫臏到了魏國，剔去孫臏的膝蓋骨並加以軟禁。後來，孫臏秘密潛回齊國，受到齊威王的重用。

公元前三四一年，魏國聯合趙國攻打韓國。韓國向齊國求援，齊威王任孫臏為軍師。兩軍交戰，互有勝負。有一天，齊軍到了一個叫馬陵的地方，那裡道路狹窄，兩旁又多阻隘，孫臏命人把一棵大樹削去樹皮，寫上："龐涓死於此樹之下"，然後佈置弓箭手夾道埋伏，吩咐一見樹下有火光即萬箭齊發。龐涓是夜抵達馬陵，他隱約看見樹上寫有字句，於是舉起火把照著看。龐涓來不及看完，齊軍已萬箭俱發。魏軍大亂，互相踐踏，死傷無數。龐涓自知智窮兵敗，心有不甘地說："成就了孫臏這小子的名望了。"於是便自刎而死。

出自《史記》

That Fellow Has Made His Name

Said when one is unconvinced of the success of others, or when one is being modest.

During the Warring States Period, Sun Bin and Pang Juan learned the arts of war from Gui Gu Zi. King Hui of the Wei State appointed Pang Juan general. Pang Juan was jealous of the talent of Sun Bin, and he tricked Sun Bin into the Wei State in the name of talking about the old days. He then wounded Sun Bin in the knee and detained him. Later, Sun Bin secretly escaped to the Qi State where he was highly thought of by King Wei of Qi.

In 341 B.C., Wei united with Zhao and attacked the Han State. Han asked Qi for help and the king of Qi appointed Sun Bin as army councilor and the two sides fought to a stalemate. One day, Qi's troops arrived at a place named Maling, where the path was narrow and rugged. Sun Bin ordered some tree bark cut down and wrote "Pang Juan will die under this tree." Then he had archers lie in wait on both sides of the path to shoot at once when they saw fire under the tree. Pang Juan arrived at Maling at night and indistinctly saw some characters on the bark. He then lit a fire to see more clearly. Before he could finish, the Qi troops let loose a hailstorm of arrows. The Wei troops were thrown into confusion and trampled each other underfoot as countless numbers died. Pang Juan realized he had lost and said unwillingly, "I have helped that puppy Sun Bin make his name." He then killed himself.

Records of the Historian

漸入佳境

jiàn rǔ jiā jìng

逐漸進入美好的境界；比喻境況逐漸好轉，或興味逐漸濃厚。

東晉畫家顧愷之是畫壇的一代宗師，他的畫論對傳統繪畫影響很大。顧愷之博學多才，兼善詩賦、書法。他的生活習慣也與別不同。據説他喜歡吃甘蔗，但每次吃甘蔗都是由上端吃起。人家覺得有趣，問他為甚麼不先吃甜的根部。他笑著説：“我先吃不怎麼甜的，逐漸吃下去，就會越吃越甜，這叫漸入佳境哩！”

出自《晉書》

漸入佳境

Gradually Entering Blissful Circumstances

Said of going from bad to good, or something becoming more and more enjoyable.

Gu Kaizhi being a master artist of the Eastern Jin Dynasty, his ideas about art greatly influenced traditional painting. A man of wide learning, Gu Kaizhi was also a skilled poet and calligrapher. His living habits were quite different from others. It was said that he liked to eat sugar cane, and he always ate from its top end. People thought this funny and asked him why he did not eat from the sweet end. He smiled, "I first eat the non-sweet part, then I'll get to the sweet part, that is gradually entering blissful circumstances."

History of the Jin Dynasty

撥雲見日

bō yún jiàn rì

撥開雲霧，看見太陽；比喻除去障礙，重見光明；也比喻沉冤得雪。

西晉尚書令衛伯玉，有一天，在朝上聽到樂廣與朝中名人雅士各抒己見。衛伯玉覺得他博學多才，見解精闢，為了加深了解他，派弟子上門造訪。弟子回來說：“樂廣這人，是人們的借鑒；見到他，就好像撥開雲霧，看見青天。”

出自《世說新語》

Dispelling the Clouds and Seeing the Sun

Said of seeing the light by removing an obstacle or restoring justice.

Wei Boyu, a minister of the Western Jin Dynasty, one day heard Yue Guang expressing his views with other celebrated people at court. Wei Boyu felt that Yue was a brilliant man of wide learning, and also had penetrating ideas. In order to know him well, he let one of his pupils visit Yue Guang. When he returned, the pupil reported, "Yue Guang is far superior to others. Seeing him is like dispelling the clouds and seeing the sun."

New Social Anecdotes

綠衣使者

lǜ yǐ shì zhě

唐玄宗給予鸚鵡的封號；現也稱郵遞員為‘綠衣使者’。

唐朝開元年間，長安富豪楊崇義突然失蹤，一個多月也不見他的蹤影。妻子劉氏便到縣衙報官，縣官派人四處查探，可是依然茫無頭緒。縣官只好親自到楊家勘查。當縣官來到後花園察看時，架上的鸚鵡忽然學著人話：“殺家主的是李弇。”李弇是楊家的鄰居，經過審訊，李弇供出了與劉氏通姦，因怕姦情暴露，便與劉氏合謀在後花園勒死了楊崇義。天網恢恢，卻被鸚鵡目睹了案發經過。

這件案子轟動了長安城，唐玄宗也知道了這件事，命人把鸚鵡傳入宮中，並封牠為‘綠衣使者’。

出自《開元天寶遺事》

The Messenger in Green

The title conferred upon a parrot by Emperor Xuanzong of the Tang Dynasty. Now referring to mailmen.

During the Kaiyuan period of the Tang Dynasty, Yang Chongyi, a rich man of Chang'an, was suddenly missing. He was not found for over a month, so his wife, surnamed Liu, reported the case to the county magistrate. The magistrate asked his men to search for him everywhere, but they found nothing. Then the magistrate himself went to the home of Yang Chongyi to investigate. When he entered the backyard garden, a parrot on the shelf suddenly spoke up, "It's Li Yan who killed my master." Li Yan was a neighbor of the Yang family. During interrogation, Li Yan admitted that he and Yang's wife Liu had committed adultery and had strangled Yang Chongyi in the garden to keep his mouth shut. What they hadn't expected was that the parrot had witnessed the whole process.

This case stirred Chang'an City, and even Emperor Xuanzong heard about it. He asked that this parrot be brought to the palace and titled it the "Messenger in Green."

Anecdotes of the Kaiyuan and Tianbao Reigns

綠葉成陰

lǜ yè chéng yīn

碧綠的樹葉已遮地成陰了；比喻女子出嫁，生兒育女，撫養後代了。

唐朝文學家杜牧，有一年遊湖州時，有一個老婦人帶著一個長得十分俊俏的十多歲少女來見他。杜牧與少女定下十年之約：如果十年以後，他不再來湖州，少女就可以嫁給別人。分手前，杜牧並給了很多錢財作為禮金。

十四年後，杜牧重臨湖州，但那少女已出嫁三年了，而且生了兩個孩子。

後來，杜牧為此寫了首《悵別》詩："自是尋春去較遲，不須惆悵怨芳時，狂風吹盡深紅色，綠葉成陰子滿枝。"

出自《唐詩記事》

Green Leaves Make a Shade

Used in reference to a young mother of many children.

Once while Du Mu, a man of letters during the Tang Dynasty, was visiting Huzhou, an old woman came to see him with a beautiful teenage girl. Du Mu became engaged to the girl and promised to return to Huzhou in ten years. If he failed to come back, he said the girl was free to marry another. Before parting from the girl, he gave her a large cash gift.

After fourteen years, when Du Mu returned to Huzhou, he found that the girl had already married three years before and had two children.

Later, Du Mu composed a poem about this called *Sorrowful Farewell*, in which he said, "*I came to look for the springtide too late, Why, therefore, should I feel forlorn while thinking back on the blooming season that year! The dark red tinge's gone with a heavy wind, The green tree has made a shade with its boughs laden with fruit.*"

Anecdotes from Tang Dynasty Poetry

銅山西崩，洛鐘東應

tóng shān xī bēng, luò zhōng dōng yìng

西邊的銅山崩潰，東面的洛鐘響應；比喻重大事件，雖相隔遙遠，都會互相影響。

孝武皇帝時，未央宮前殿的銅鐘無緣無故響了起來，歷時三日三夜不止。孝武帝詔問太史待詔王朔這是甚麼原因。王朔說："這樣的異常反應，可能是戰亂的預兆。"孝武帝轉而問東方朔，東方朔說："臣聽說銅是山的兒子，山是銅的母親。以陰陽氣類而論，母體出現異象，兒子會有所感應，由於有山崩的預兆，所以銅鐘先鳴。"

後來，南郡太守上書孝武帝說，山崩延綿二十餘里。

出自《世說新語》

Tongshan Mountain Falls in the West and Luo Bronze Bell Responds in the East

Meaning significant events will produce an effect on each other though they may be separated by great distance.

Once during the reign of Emperor Xiaowu of the Western Han Dynasty, the bronze bell in the front hall of the Weiyang Palace rang for three whole days and nights for no reason at all. Emperor Xiaowu asked Wang Shuo, an Expectant Grand Scribe, why the bell rang. Wang Shuo answered, "This abnormal phenomenon is probably a sign of wars."Emperor Xiaowu then asked Dongfang Shuo, and he answered, "I heard that bronze is the son of the mountain and the mountain is the mother of bronze. If something is going to happen to the mother, the son will respond to it first. The bronze bell rang as the sign of an avalanche." Soon after, the magistrate of Nanjun reported to Emperor Xiaowu that an avalanche had occurred stretching over ten meters.

New Social Anecdotes

嘔心瀝血

ōu xīn lì xuè

形容創作時窮思苦索，費盡心血。

唐朝傑出詩人李賀，雖然在仕途上一直不得意，但無損他的聲名。李賀十幾歲時就被稱為‘東京才子’。他所作的詩善於溶鑄詞采，而且好用神話傳說，創造出新奇瑰麗的意境。

李賀每次外遊，想到好的詩句時，馬上記下來，放到書囊裡。晚間回到家裡時，母親看見書囊裡裝滿了詩句，很心疼地說：“我的兒子是要把心嘔出來才算是休止啊！”

出自《李長吉小傳》

嘔心瀝血

To Vomit Out the Heart and Drip Blood

Used in reference to someone racking his brains to create literary works.

Li He, a great poet of the Tang Dynasty, though not successful in his official career, was still famous for his literary works. Li He was known as "a gifted scholar of the Eastern Capital" while still a teenager. He composed brilliant poems and preferred to use fairy tales to create his novel and magnificent works.

When Li He was out and thought of a great line, he would write it down at once and put it in his bookbag. Back home one day in the evening, his mother, seeing that Li He had written so many lines, said lovingly and sympathetically, "You won't stop until you vomit your heart out."

A Brief Biography of Li Changji

暮夜無知

mù yè wú zhī

黑夜裡無人知道；比喻暗中賄賂。

東漢大臣楊震，從少好學，博覽群經，當時被稱為‘關西孔子’。他為官清廉，執法公正嚴明。

有一次，他路過昌邑，縣令王密是他推薦的秀才。王密當天夜裡，帶著十斤黃金暗中送給楊震。楊震很不高興地說：“我們是老朋友了，我瞭解你，可是你卻不瞭解我，為何如此呢？”王密說：“深夜裡不會有人知道的。”楊震大聲說：“天知、神知、我知、你知。何謂無知！”

楊震一生剛正不阿，多次上疏切諫權貴的貪侈驕橫。後來被中常侍樊豐所誣罷官，憤而自殺。

出自《後漢書》

No One Knows in the Dead of the Night

Said of secretly making a bribe.

Yang Zhen, a senior official during the Eastern Han Dynasty, was called "Confucius west of Tongguan Pass" for his great learning. He was known to be upright and impartial in his judgement.

One day Yang Zhen passed by Changyi, where the county magistrate was Wang Mi, a scholar recommended by him for the post. That night, Wang Mi went to visit him and wanted to give him ten catties of gold. Yang Zhen said unhappily, "We are old friends. I know what kind of person you are, but why don't you know me?" Wang Mi said, "Nobody will know in the dead of night." Yang Zhen replied loudly, "Heaven knows, God knows, you know and I know. How can you say nobody knows?"

Yang Zhen was outspoken and frank, and many times he sent memorials impeaching corrupt and evil high officials. Later, he was framed up by Fan Feng, a palace attendant, and was dismissed from office. In a fit of bitterness, he ended his life.

History of the Later Han Dynasty

撲朔迷離

pū shù mí lí

模糊不清，難辨雌雄；現比喻事情錯綜複雜，不易辨認。

人們在辨別兔子雌雄的時候，常用的方法是拎住兔子的耳朵懸空起來，如兔子四腳亂蹬，是為‘撲朔’，這隻就是雄兔。如果兔子雙眼眯起來，叫作‘迷離’，這就是雌兔。可是，兔子在地上奔跑時，那就很難辨認哪隻是雌哪隻是雄了。

古時候，木蘭女扮男裝代替父親上戰場打仗，這一去就是十年，復員回鄉後，又重新回復女兒身的裝扮。昔日的戰友這時才知道木蘭原來是個女子，均被木蘭的孝心所感動。所以，在南北朝時北朝的民歌《木蘭詩》裡說：“雄兔腳撲朔，雌兔眼迷離，雙兔傍地走，安能辨我是雄雌？”

出自《木蘭詩》

撲朔迷離

Feet Kicking and Eyes Narrowed

Unable to distinguish male from female. Also said of something that is complicated and confusing.

To tell whether a rabbit is male or female, people always seize the rabbit by the ear and lift it off the ground. If the rabbit kicks with all four feet, it must be a male; and if the rabbit narrows its eyes, it must be a female. But when the rabbit is running along the ground, you cannot tell its sex.

In ancient times, there was a girl called Mu Lan who disguised herself as a man and went to war on her father's behalf. After ten years of fighting on the battlefield, she was demobilized home and changed into woman's clothes. Until then her battle companions did not know she was a girl, and now they all were moved by her love for her father. *Ode to Mu Lan*, a folk song during the Northern and Southern Dynasties, goes like this, "*The male rabbit will kick his feet, And the female rabbit will narrow her eyes. While two rabbits are running on the ground, Who can tell which is which?*"

Ode to Mu Lan

談笑自若

tán xiào zì ruò

有說有笑，和平日一樣；形容在緊急意外的情況下，非常從容鎮定。

曹操自赤壁戰敗後，向匯陵撤退。但被孫權、劉備聯軍乘勝追擊，一路追到南郡。南郡的位置與夷陵互為犄角。當時的吳國將領甘寧建議周瑜先取夷陵，再攻南郡。於是，周瑜派甘寧率軍直逼夷陵，與魏國守將曹洪激戰，終於攻下了夷陵。

第二天，曹洪糾合了曹仁、牛金兵力五千餘人，築起高台，圍城攻打。曹軍在高台上向城中射箭，殺傷了不少吳兵。很多將士都懼怕起來，唯獨甘寧談笑自若，和平時一樣，率軍堅守城池。

後來，甘寧終於堅守到周瑜派兵救援，擊退了魏軍的進攻。

出自《三國志》

Talking and Laughing As If Nothing Had Happened

To be completely at ease. Also said of someone who remains calm and collected at a critical moment.

After Cao Cao was defeated in Chibi, he led his army in retreat toward Huiling. However, the allied forces of Sun Quan and Liu Bei continued their triumphant pursuit all the way to Nanjun. The cities of Nanjun and Yiling were next to each other, so Gan Ning, the Wu Kingdom general, suggested to the field commander Zhou Yu that they capture Yiling first and then Nanjun. Then Gan Ning was sent to fight against Cao Hong, Wei Kingdom's garrison commander at the city of Yiling. After a fierce battle, Gan Ning captured Yiling.

The next day, Cao Hong mustered Cao Ren and Niu Jin's forces, more than five thousand strong, and constructed a high platform from which they launched an attack on the city. Cao Hong's troops shot arrows from the platform and killed or wounded many of Wu's soldiers. Many of Wu's soldiers were frightened but Gan Ning remained his usual self, talking and laughing as if nothing were happening.

Gan Ning held fast to his position until the forces sent by Zhou Yu came to his relief and repulsed the enemy attack.

History of the Three Kingdoms

賣刀買牛

mài dāo mǎi niú

賣掉刀劍買耕牛；比喻改惡從善或指棄武務農，解甲歸田。

漢宣帝時，渤海地區連續幾年災荒，老百姓被逼鋌而走險，農民也紛起暴動。

當時渤海太守龔遂苦口婆心地勸告農民回到田裡耕作，誘導老百姓賣掉刀劍去買耕牛，共同奮鬥，渡過難關。經過龔遂的悉心治理，艱苦經營，渤海地區的災荒得到了紓緩，社會治安也好轉了。

出自《漢書》

Selling the Knife to Buy Cattle

Said of turning over a new leaf, or taking off one's armor and going home to work on the land.

During the reign of Emperor Xuandi of the Han Dynasty, the Bohai area had suffered famine for several years running and the farmers had no way out but to riot.

Gong Sui, then governor of Bohai, did his best to convince the farmers to go back to the fields, sell their knives and swords, and buy cattle to get through the difficult period. Through Gong Sui's careful administration, the famine in the Bohai area was finally alleviated and social peace was restored.

History of the Han Dynasty

戮力同心

lù lì tóng xīn

團結一致，齊心合力。

夏朝的末代君主桀是一個荒淫無道的暴君，整日裡縱情享樂，無心治理朝政，致使政治腐敗，國勢衰弱。

夏朝東面的諸侯國商，在君主湯的任用賢人、勵精圖治下，國力日漸雄厚。湯不問出身，重用了據說是奴隸出身的伊尹。在伊尹的輔助下，出征十一次，攻取了鄰近的葛國及夏的盟國韋、顧、昆吾等國。商的國力空前強大，滅亡夏朝的條件已經成熟。在出征滅夏前夕，商湯在誓師文告中說："夏桀無道，天意決定他要滅亡，上天派來賢人伊尹輔政，戮力同心，以治天下。"終於商湯一舉攻滅了夏，建立了商朝。

出自《墨子》

Pulling Together and Working with One Heart and One Mind

Said of cooperative efforts.

Jie, the last emperor of the Xia Dynasty, was a tyrant who indulged himself in sensual pleasures and gave no thought to governing the country. As a result, corruption prevailed everywhere in the country and the nation's strength became weakened.

At this time Tang, the ruler of Shang, a vassal state to the east of Xia, was exerting himself to make Shang prosperous and put Yi Yin, said to be a former slave, in an important position. With the assistance of Yi Yin, Tang led his army on eleven expeditions and occupied the neighboring state of Ge, and those of Xia's allies the Wei, Gu and Kunwu. Now, Shang was extremely powerful and was ready to end the Xia Dynasty. Before his troops set out, Tang said in his proclamation that "Jie of the Xia Dynasty is fatuous and tyrannical. Xia's extinction is the will of Heaven. God has sent Yi Yin, a person of virtue, to assist us. Let's pull together and work with one heart and one mind to bring order to the whole world." And at last, Tang defeated Xia and established the Shang Dynasty.

The Book of Mo Zi

黎丘丈人

lí qiū zhàng rén

黎丘的老人；比喻受假象迷惑，不辨真相而犯錯。

從前，在黎丘（今河南省虞城縣北）有一種奇鬼，喜歡幻化別人的子侄、兄弟的模樣。有一天，一個老人喝醉了酒，在回家的路上，黎丘奇鬼幻化成老人的兒子，攙扶他回家。老人醒來後，與兒子說起，才知道受了奇鬼的愚弄。老人說：“嘻，明天我去喝酒，叫我碰上就一劍刺死它。”

老人第二天又喝醉了酒，兒子耽心父親出事，便在老人的回路上接他。老人見到兒子，一時醉眼昏花，不辨真偽，一劍把自己的兒子刺死了。

出自《呂氏春秋》

The Old Man at Liqiu

Said of someone who is unable to distinguish the genuine from the false.

Once there was a ghost in Liqiu (north of present-day Yucheng County in Henan Province), who liked to transform himself into other people's sons or brothers. One day, an old man got drunk and on his way home, the ghost took the form of his son and helped him back to his home. When the old man sobered up and saw his son, he realized that he had been strung along by the ghost and said angrily, "Tomorrow I'll be out for some drink. I'll kill him with my sword when I meet him again."

The next day, the old man was drunk again. His son worried about his father and went out to meet him on his way home. When the old man caught sight of his son, he could not see clearly and stabbed his son to death.

The Discourses of Lü Buwei

銷聲匿跡

xiāo shēng nì jī

不出聲，隱藏行跡；比喻秘密到一邊藏匿起來，不吭聲，不露面。

唐朝的時候，有一個姓宗的人是四川節度使陳敬瑄年輕時的好朋友。兩人一同吃喝玩樂，遊山玩水。可是，有一次兩人為了爭奪一個女子鬧翻了，從此成為仇人。

兩人絕交後，陳敬瑄仕途得意，官運亨通，當了四川節度使。

後來，長安發生叛亂，不少人從長安來到了四川避難。姓宗的也到了四川。但四川是陳敬瑄管轄的，姓宗的害怕陳找他報仇，於是便居無定所，到處藏匿，不敢現身。誰知，陳敬瑄早已派人四處明查暗訪，終於把他找出來殺了。

出自《北夢瑣言》

Keep Silent and Vanish Without Leaving a Trace Behind

Said of someone who hides himself and disappears from the scene.

During the Tang Dynasty, there was a man named Zong who had been a good friend of Chen Jingxuan when they were young. The two often went traveling and sought other pleasures together. However, they eventually became enemies after a fight for a woman's favor.

After they broke off their relationship, Chen Jingxuan became very successful in his official career and was named military commissioner of Sichuan. When there was a riot in Chang'an, many Chang'an people found refuge in Sichuan, including Chen's old friend Zong. Zong knew that Sichuan was under the supervision of Chen Jingxuan and was afraid Chen might take revenge. So he constantly changed his residence and dared not appear in public. However, Chen Jingxuan had already sent his men out to every corner of the city to look for Zong. When they finally ferreted Zong out, they killed him.

Trifling Words of Northern Dream

舉棋不定

jǔ qí bù dìng

拿起棋子，不知下哪一著好；比喻臨事優柔寡斷，拿不定主意。

春秋時，衛國大夫孫文子和寧惠子聯手推翻了衛獻公的統治，把持了衛國朝政，而衛獻公逃到齊國避難去了。

寧惠子雖然成功驅逐了衛獻公，但他內心卻感到驅逐國君乃有罪之舉，所以臨死時，囑咐兒子寧悼子要把衛獻公接回來。

儘管衛獻公知道要接他回國的消息後，許諾保證回國後不問國事，仍由寧悼子掌管朝政，但是，大夫們仍一致反對衛獻公回來，認為他的許諾是口是心非。大夫大叔儀對寧悼子說："你處理國家大事，有如下棋的人拿著棋子猶豫不決，不知下哪一著好，這怎麼能戰勝對手呢？對待國君這樣的大事，一時把他驅逐，一時又要接他回來，將來難逃殺身之禍。"

寧悼子不聽大夫們的勸告，讓衛獻公復位了。過了一段時間，衛獻公施展手段，把寧悼子全家殺光斬絕。

出自《左傳》

Hesitate at Making a Chess Move

Shilly-shally

Said of someone who vacillates and is uncertain what to do next.

During the Spring and Autumn Period, senior officials Sun Wen

Zi and Ning Hui Zi joined hands in overthrowing the rule of Duke Xian of the Wei State. Duke Xian then fled to the state of Qi to take refuge.

After expelling Duke Xian, Ning Hui Zi often felt guilty about what he had done, and upon his death he asked his son, Ning Dao Zi, to fetch Duke Xian back to Wei.

When Duke Xian heard the news, he promised that he would not involve himself in state affairs and that the state would continue to be run by Ning Dao Zi. However, not all the senior officials believed Duke Xian's words and were in disagreement about his return. Minister Da Shu Yi said to Ning Dao Zi, "When handling state affairs, how can you hesitate as though you were playing chess and didn't know what move to make next? On such a big decision involving the duke, you first expelled him and then you want to welcome him back, this will be very dangerous for you."

Despite this advice, Ning Dao Zi restored Duke Xian's position. But after a period of time, Duke Xian carried out his intrigues and killed the entire Ning Dao Zi family.

Zuo Qiuming's Chronicles

舉棋不定

獨當一面

dú dǎng yī miàn

獨立擔當一個方面的重任；形容精明能幹，有超卓的領導才能。

楚漢相爭時，劉邦率領大軍從漢中向東攻打項羽。戰事初期，劉邦攻下了彭城。但被項羽迅速集結兵力，大舉反攻，打得漢軍傷亡慘重。劉邦因此而悶悶不樂，意志消沉。

有一天，他對張良説："誰能打敗項羽，我就把函谷關以東的地方送給他。"張良説："黥布勇猛無倫，而且與項羽一向不和；彭越正起兵反對項羽，可以借用他們的力量。至於你所統率的將領，只有韓信能獨當一面承當重任。你把關東的地方分送給他們，這樣就可以戰勝項羽了。"

後來，楚漢相爭中，劉邦取得了勝利，主要依靠了韓信、黥布、彭越三人的力量。

出自《史記》

Taking Sole Charge on Any Battlefront

Said of someone who is intelligent and capable in a leadership position.

During the war between the states of Chu and Han, Liu Bang led his army to fight eastward against Xiang Yu from the Hanzhong area. At the beginning of the war, Liu Bang occupied Pengcheng. However, Xiang Yu quickly mustered his army for a large-scale counterattack that brought heavy losses to the Han army. Liu Bang was unhappy and depressed.

One day, Liu Bang said to Zhang Liang, "I'll give the land east of the Hangu Pass as a gift to the one who can defeat Xiang Yu." Zhang Liang said, "Qing Bu is very brave and on bad terms with Xiang Yu; Peng Yue has staged a rebellion against Xiang Yu. You may be able to take advantage of their forces. As for your generals, only Han Xin can take charge on his own on any one of the battlefronts. You'd better give the land east of the pass to these three and you will win the war."

And Liu Bang won the war with the help of Han Xin, Qing Bu, and Peng Yue.

Records of the Historian

澠池之功

miǎn chí zhī gōng

在澠池立下功勞；形容為國家立下巨大的功勞。

戰國時，秦王邀請趙王到澠池會飲，趙王由藺相如陪同赴約。

當秦王酒酣耳熱時，秦王說："我聽聞趙王擅長音樂，請奏瑟助興吧。"趙王依言奏瑟。這時，秦御史寫上："某年月日，秦王與趙王會飲，秦王命令趙王鼓瑟。"藺相如針鋒相對地說："趙王也聽說秦王善為秦聲，請奏盆缻以相娛樂。"秦王非常憤怒，拒絕了藺相如。藺相如堅毅地說："大王不奏樂，五步之內，我以頸血濺污大王了。"秦王沒有辦法，只好奏樂了。藺相如即命趙御史錄道："某年月日，秦王為趙王擊缻。"接著，秦國的大臣說："請趙王以十五座城池為秦王祝壽。"藺相如毫不示弱地說："請以秦國的咸陽為趙王祝壽。"

藺相如的機智勇敢，滅了秦王的威風，使趙王全身而退。

出自《史記》

Rendering Meritorious Service at Mianchi

Used in reference to one who has performed outstanding service for his country.

During the Warring States Period, the king of the state of Zhao, accompanied by Lin Xiangru, was invited by the king of the state of Qin to a dinner at Mianchi.

The king of Qin was in a good mood after a few cups, and he said to the king of Zhao, "I heard that you are very good at playing the zither, please play it for our entertainment." The king of Zhao obliged and proceeded to play. At that moment, the royal scribe of Qin wrote, "On such a day in such a month in such a year, the king of Qin ordered the king of Zhao to play the zither for him." Lin Xiangru, paying tit for tat, said at once, "The king of Zhao also heard that the king of Qin is good at playing the fou pitcher. Please play it for us to enjoy." The king of Qin was very angry and refused to play. Lin Xiangru said unyieldingly, "I am only five steps from you. If you don't play, I can bespatter you with blood." The king of Qin then had no choice but to play. Lin Xiangru then asked the royal scribe of Zhao to write, "On such a day in such a month in such a year, the king of Qin played the fou pitcher for the king of Zhao." After this, one official of Qin said, "Let the king of Zhao give fifteen cities to the king of Qin as a birthday gift." Lin Xiangru was not to be outdone, and said, "Then please celebrate the king of Zhao's birthday with Qin's capital Xianyang as gift." Lin Xiangru's wisdom and bravery ran the king of Qin down, and the king of Zhao returned to his state with all his faculties intact.

Records of the Historian

錢可通神

qián kě tōng shén

金錢可以買通鬼神；形容金錢的魔力，可以買通一切。

唐朝的時候，有一個叫張延的官員，試圖過問一件大案，派人嚴密偵緝。有一天，他看見書桌上有一小帖“錢三萬貫，請不要過問此案”。他憤怒地把帖子擲在地上。

第二天，書桌上又有小帖“十萬貫”。張延不再過問了。他的子弟覺得奇怪，向他試探原因。張延說：“十萬貫錢，可以通神矣，無不可辦的事情，我恐怕惹禍上身，不得不放手了。”

出自《幽閑鼓吹》

錢可通神

Money Can Move Even the Gods

Money Makes the Mare Go

Money is so powerful that everything can be bought.

During the Tang Dynasty, an official named Zhang Yan attempted to involve himself in a big case and sent agents out to investigate. One day, he saw a note on his desk which said, "Here are thirty thousand strings of cash. Don't bother yourself with this case any more." He angrily threw the note to the ground.

The next day, there was another note on the desk saying, "One hundred thousand strings of cash." After reading the note, Zhang Yan stopped his investigation. His followers were curious and asked him why. Zhang Yan answered, "One hundred thousand strings of cash can move even the gods. I'm afraid I will stir up trouble if I don't give it up."

Random Talks in Leisure Time

鬨堂大笑

hōng táng dà xiào

形容滿屋子的人同時大笑。

北宋文學家歐陽修在《歸田錄》裡記載了一段“鬨堂大笑”的趣事：馮相、和相兩人是同僚，兩人的性情，一個是詼諧、風趣；一個是急性子。有一天，和相看到馮相穿了雙新靴子，問道：“你這新靴子，花了多少錢？”馮相舉起左腳說：“九百。”和相急忙轉身對下人說：“為甚麼我的靴子要花一千八百？”隨即責罵了下人一頓。這時，馮相慢慢舉起右腳說：“這也是九百。”在座的人都鬨堂大笑起來。

出自《歸田錄》

Setting the Whole Room Roaring

Said of a scene ringing with laughter.

Ouyang Xiu, a man of letters of the Northern Song Dynasty, recorded an anecdote in one of his works:

Feng Xiang and He Xiang were colleagues. One was humorous and the other was impetuous. One day, He Xiang saw Feng Xiang wearing a pair of new boots and asked, "How much did your new boots cost?" Feng Xiang raised his left foot and said, "Nine hundred." He Xiang turned to his servant and said hastily, "Why did my boots cost eighteen hundred?" Then he began to scold his servant. At that moment, Feng Xiang raised his right foot slowly and said, "This one also cost nine hundred." Everyone in the room roared with laughter.

Records After Returning to the Farm

縱橫捭闔

zòng héng bǎi hé

形容運用手段在政治、外交上進行分化瓦解或拉攏。

戰國時，張儀、蘇秦都曾在鬼谷子門下學藝，但兩人卻有不同的政治主張。後來，師兄弟二人憑著學來的本領，游說、往來於各國之間。

當時七國爭雄，蘇秦說服了六國‘合縱’，聯結起來，抵禦強大的秦國，阻止了秦國向東擴展。張儀本來是魏國的貴族後代，他任秦國相時，運用了‘連橫’術，游說了六國分別與秦國結盟，逼使魏國獻出上郡，瓦解了齊國與楚國的聯盟。

六國後來因彼此猜疑，互不團結，被秦國各個擊破，統一了天下。

出自《戰國策》

Lengthwise and Breadthwise, Opening and Closing

Said of political and diplomatic tact.

During the Warring States Period, Zhang Yi and Su Qin were disciples of Gui Gu Zi, but the two held different political views. Upon completion of their studies the two disciples went canvassing among the states. At that time there were seven states vying for supremacy. Su Qin succeeded in uniting six smaller states to form an alliance against the state of Qin in order to stop the dominant and powerful Qin's expansion eastward. Zhang Yi was descended from the nobility of the state of Wei. While serving as the prime minister of Qin, he successfully undermined the solidarity of the six smaller states, all of which then formed separate alliances with Qin. Thus the state of Wei was forced to surrender Shangjun Prefecture, and the alliance between the states of Qi and Chu disintegrated.

The six states were suspicious of each other from then on, and Qin crushed them one by one, finally unifying the whole country.

Anecdotes of the Warring States

斷頭將軍

duàn tóu jiāng jūn

寧可斷頭的將軍；比喻寧死不屈，堅決抵抗的將領。

三國時，劉備率軍攻打四川的劉璋。當時，嚴顏是防守江州的太守。張飛領兵進攻江州時，嚴顏帶領將士拒降抵抗。

後來，張飛攻破了江州城池，活捉了嚴顏。當張飛看到嚴顏被押解來時，粗聲粗氣地說："我大軍壓境，你不趕快投降，竟然還要抵抗？"嚴顏說："你真是粗暴無理，侵奪我江州，竟還要我投降？我這裡只有斷頭的將軍，哪有投降的將軍。"張飛暴跳如雷，喝令部下把他砍殺。嚴顏毫不畏懼地說："要殺就殺吧，發甚麼脾氣。"張飛聽後，覺得嚴顏是個硬漢子，親自把他放了，並且和他交了朋友。

出自《三國志》

A General Who Fears Not the Loss of His Head

Said of a general who resists the enemy unwaveringly.

During the Three Kingdoms Period, Liu Bei led his army in an attack against Liu Zhang in Sichuan. Zhang Fei, a general under Liu Bei, then launched an assault against Jiangzhou Prefecture, but met with resistance from Yan Yan, the governor of Jiangzhou who refused to surrender.

Later, Zhang Fei occupied the city and captured Yan Yan alive. When Zhang Fei saw Yan Yan arriving under escort, he said to him in a deep, gruff voice, "When my massive force swooped down on you, why did you bother yourself with resistance instead of surrendering?" Yan Yan answered, "You are an unreasonable person. You've invaded our land, how can you ask me to surrender? There's a general here who would rather lose his head than surrender." Zhang Fei flew into a rage and ordered Yan Yan beheaded. Yan Yan said, without showing a trace of fear, "Do anything you want. You needn't be so angry." By these words, Zhang Fei recognized that Yan Yan was a true man. He set him free and even became good friends with him.

History of the Three Kingdoms

斷鶴續鳧

duàn hè xù fú

截斷鶴的長腿接肢在鳧（野鴨）的短腿上；比喻不按自然規律辦事。

從前有一個人，看到鶴的腿特別長，鳧的腿卻很短。他忽發奇想：如果把鶴的長腿截去一段，接續到鳧的短腿上，這不是又好看，又好用嗎？結果，鶴和鳧既不能飛，也不能走。

莊子議論說：“天生長的，不是多餘；天生短的，不是不足。鳧的腿雖然短，給牠接長，牠要懮傷得物無所用；鶴的腿雖然長，給牠截短，牠要悲哀失掉了所長。”

出自《莊子》

Shortening the Leg of a Crane to Lengthen the Leg of a Wild Duck

Alluding to going against the natural law.

Once upon a time, there was a man who suddenly got an idea when he saw the extremely long legs of a crane and the short legs of a wild duck. He then shortened the legs of the crane and lengthened those of the wild duck, thinking it would be good and convenient for both of them. As a result, neither the crane nor the wild duck could ever fly or walk again.

Zhuang Zi (Chuang Tzu) said, "If the crane is born long-legged, it is necessary; if the wild duck is born short-legged, it is not a shortcoming. If you lengthen the leg of the wild duck, he will be sad because the leg will be useless; if you shorten the leg of the crane, he will be sad because he will have lost his strength."

The Book of Zhuang Zi

藍田生玉

lān tián shēng yù

藍田出產美玉；比喻賢父生賢子。

東吳將領諸葛謹，字子瑜，是諸葛亮的哥哥。他甚受孫權的重用。有一次，孫權設宴，諸葛謹帶同六歲大的兒子諸葛恪赴宴。席間，孫權興致甚高，便命人牽來一頭驢子，在驢的長臉上寫了‘諸葛子瑜’四個字。眾人看了都捧腹大笑（因諸葛謹的臉長得特別長）。這時，諸葛恪也拿起筆來，在‘諸葛子瑜’後面添寫了‘之驢’二字，變成了‘諸葛子瑜之驢’。孫權見他如此聰明伶俐，把驢子賞賜給他。

又有一次，孫權問諸葛恪：“你父親和你叔父相比，哪個高明呢？”諸葛恪回答道：“當然是我父親高明，因為他懂得選擇明主。”孫權聽了，大為高興。

孫權有感於諸葛恪的年少英才，對諸葛謹說：“藍田產美玉，此言不虛。”

出自《三國志》

藍田生玉

Jade Produced in Lantian

Said of children born of great parents.

Zhuge Jin, styled Ziyu, was the brother of Zhuge Liang and a general of the Wu Kingdom, who was placed in an important position by King Sun Quan. Once, Zhuge Jin went with his six-year-old son Zhuge Ke to a banquet given by Sun Quan. During the meal, Sun Quan was of good cheer and asked an attendant to bring in a donkey. He then wrote "Zhuge Ziyu" on the donkey's long face. All the people at the banquet broke into laughter because Zhuge Jin had a uniquely long face. Just then, Zhuge Ke took a brush and added "'s donkey" to his father's name. Sun Quan thought the boy was smart and gave the donkey to him as a gift. Another time, Sun Quan asked Zhuge Ke, "Who is wiser, your father or your uncle?" "My father, of course," Zhuge Ke answered, "because he chose a wise master." Sun Quan was quite happy with these words.

Thinking of Zhuge Ke's wisdom at such a young age, Sun Quan said to Zhuge Jin, "It's true that beautiful jade is produced in Lantian."

History of the Three Kingdoms

藥籠中物

yào lóng zhōng wù

藥籠中儲備的藥材；比喻儲備有用的人才。

唐朝的時候，元行沖對狄仁傑說："部下能夠隨時為自己效力，就好像富有人家善於儲積自己的資產。例如，肉脯、臘肉、魚肉脯、乾肉等，用於膳食；參、朮、芝、桂用來預防疾病。在你門下已有許多人才了，你願意把我也備為一種藥石嗎？"狄仁傑笑著說："你正是我的藥籠中物，不可一日無也。"

出自《新唐書》

Things in the Medicine Kit

Used in reference to talent kept in reserve.

During the Tang Dynasty, Yuan Xingchong said to Di Renjie, "Subordinates ready to serve their masters at all times are like rich people storing their property. For instance, the rich will store dried pork, cured meat, and dried fish for future use, and ginseng, atractylodes rhizome, glossy ganoderma, cassia and other herbs to prevent disease. There are already many people serving you. Do you want me to be one of the herbs?" Di Renjie said with a smile, "You are one of the herbs in my medicine kit. I can not do without you."

New History of the Tang Dynasty

寵辱不驚

chǒng rǔ bù jīng

受寵或受辱都不驚詫；形容對得失不介懷，置之度外。

唐高宗初年，盧承慶負責考核百官政績的工作。有一個負責運輸的官員，因遇到大風浪，運糧船沉溺了，損失了一大批糧食。盧承慶評他的政績為中下。這位官員沒吭一聲，也沒有爭辯就退下去了。盧承慶接著説："遇到天災，不是人力所能抗拒，政績評為中等。"但這位官員仍然神色自若，既不喜形於色，也沒有慚愧之言。盧承慶讚許道："寵辱不驚，政績應考中上。如果百官都像他這樣就好了。"

出自《新唐書》

Not Moved by Honor or Disgrace

Said of someone who is unmoved by either gain or loss.

In the first years of the reign of Emperor Gaozong of the Tang Dynasty, Lu Chengqing was in charge of supervising the work of all officials. Once a ship loaded with grain sank during a storm at sea. Lu Chengqing evaluated the work of the official in charge of transportation as below standard. Hearing of this judgement, the transportation official then went back home without comment. Lu Chengqing then reconsidered, and said, "Man can't stop natural disasters. Your work should be evaluated as passable." However, the official remained indifferent, showing neither gratitude nor shame. Lu Chengqing said with approval, "Your work should now be evaluated as above the average because you have remained undisturbed by both honor and disgrace. If only all the other officials were like you!"

New History of the Tang Dynasty

懸駝就石

xuán tuó jiù shí

懸掛駱駝來遷就磨刀石；形容做事情本末倒置、愚昧可笑。

古時候，有一個人得到一頭死了的駱駝。他剝駱駝皮時嫌刀子鈍，剛好樓上有一塊磨刀石，於是他一會兒跑到樓上磨刀，一會兒又下樓剝駝皮，如此跑上跑落，他感到不勝其煩。他為了就近磨刀，費了很大的氣力，把駱駝搬到樓上掛起來，而不是把磨刀石搬下來。

出自《百喻經》

懸駝就石

Hanging the Camel Up To Be Near to the Whetstone

Said of putting the incidental before the fundamental.

In ancient times, there was a man who had a dead camel. While skinning the camel, he found that his knife was blunt, so he went upstairs to sharpen it on the whetstone and then went downstairs to continue his work. After a while he found that going upstairs and downstairs every now and again was too troublesome. So in order to be near to the whetstone, he tried very hard to move the camel up the stairs, instead of moving the whetstone downstairs.

Sutra of One Hundred Parables

響遏行雲

xiǎng è xíng yǔn

聲音高入雲霄，把飄動著的雲彩也阻止了；形容歌聲響亮有力，悅耳動聽。

戰國時，有一個名叫薛譚的人，拜秦青為師，學習唱歌。他學習了一段時間，以為把秦青的全部技巧都學到手了，便辭別秦青要回去了。

秦青也不挽留他，在郊外設置酒食為他餞行。酒過三巡，秦青打著拍子，唱著悲歌。歌聲振動了林木，歌聲響遏了行雲，天空中流動著的雲彩被歌聲止住不動了。薛譚這時才明白自己只學了些皮毛。於是，他連忙請求再隨秦青學藝。從此以後，薛譚終身不再自負了。

出自《列子》

The Music Stops the Passing Clouds

Descriptive of a beautiful singing voice which can stop passers-by.

During the Warring States Period, there was a man named Xue Tan who took Qin Qing as his singing teacher. After studying for some time, he thought he had learned all the singing techniques his teacher had to offer, and Qin Qing intended to dismiss him. Before doing so, however, he gave him a farewell dinner in the suburbs. After three drinks, Qin Qing began singing a sad song. His voice was so beautiful that it stopped even the passing clouds. Until then, Xue Tan didn't realize that what he had so far learned was just a smattering, and he hastened to beg Qin Qing to remain his teacher. From then on, Xue Tan never thought so highly of himself.

The Book of Lie Zi

顧名思義

gù míng sī yì

看到名稱，就聯想到含義。

三國時的王昶，為人正直、謙虛。他給兒子、侄子起名字都用含有謙實意義的字和詞。他給侄子起的名字為：王默，字處靜；王沈，字處道。他的兒子起名為：王渾，字玄沖；王深，字道沖。

有一次，他寫信給侄子、兒子說："我給你們起這樣的名字，用意是要求你們看到名字，就要顧名思義，想著裡面的意義，經常約束自己的行為，不要行差踏錯。"

出自《三國志》

Thinking What a Title or Name Implies

Seeing the name of a thing, one thinks of its meaning.

During the Three Kingdoms Period, there was an honest and modest man named Wang Chang. He gave his nephews and sons names which all had a meaning of modesty. He named his two nephews Wang Mo, styled Chujing, and Wang Chen, styled Chudao; and he named his sons Wang Hun, styled Xuanchong, and Wang Shen, styled Daochong.

Once, in a letter to his nephews and sons he wrote, "The reason I gave you such names is that I want you always think of their meaning, so that you may restrain yourself and avoid making mistakes."

History of the Three Kingdoms

鷗鳥不下

ōu niǎo bù xià

鷗鳥不肯飛落下來；比喻察覺別人有相害之心，加以防範。

古時候，海上有一個喜愛鷗鳥的人，每天都出海與鷗鳥玩遊。每次總有百多隻鷗鳥飛來，其時，人鳥共樂，玩得忘乎所以。

有一天，父親對他說："我聽說鷗鳥喜歡與你玩樂，明天和你一同出海，你引牠們下來，讓我耍弄一番。"第二天，父子兩人來到海上，但見飛來的鷗鳥只在天空盤旋飛舞，好像識破了他們的奸詐，不肯下來。

出自《列子》

The Seagulls Won't Come Down

Said of being on guard against someone who means harm.

In ancient times, there was a man living by the sea who loved seagulls very much and went playing with them by the shore everyday. Hundreds of seagulls flew to him and they all had much fun.

One day, his father said to him, "I heard the seagulls like to play with you. I'd like to go down to the sea with you tomorrow. Then you should induce them to come down so I can make fun of them." The next day, father and son went down to the sea. However, it seemed that the seagulls had seen through this trick, for they all wheeled in the air above them and wouldn't come down.

The Book of Lie Zi

囊螢映雪

náng yíng yìng xuě

夏天把螢火蟲裝在袋中以及冬天利用雪光來照明讀書；形容刻苦攻讀，勤奮不倦。

晉代人車胤，恭勤不倦，博學多才。但他小時候家境貧苦，時常沒有錢買燈油。於是，他在夏天裡，捉來幾十隻螢火蟲，裝在白布袋中用來照明讀書。

孫康也是晉代人，自幼家貧，在冬天夜裡，利用白雪的反光照著看書。後來，‘囊螢’、‘映雪’形成了‘囊螢映雪’的成語。

出自《晉書》、《宋齊語》

Bagged Fireflies and the Reflected Light of the Snow

Descriptive of someone who pursues knowledge in difficult circumstances.

Che Yin of the Jin Dynasty was a great scholar of wide learning. During his childhood, his family was so poor that they sometimes couldn't afford lamp-oil. On summer nights, Che Yin caught dozens of fireflies and bagged them so that he could read by their light.

Also during the Jin Dynasty, there was a man named Sun Kang who lived in poverty when he was young. On winter evenings, he read books by the reflected light of the snow.

History of the Jin Dynasty and
The Book of the Song and Qi Dynasties

附錄
APPENDICES

英文索引 273
English Index

漢語拼音索引 283
Chinese Phonetic Alphabet Index

引用書目 291
Bibliography

中國歷史年代簡表 295
A Chronology of Chinese Dynasties

漢語拼音發音指南 299
Guide to Chinese Phonetic Alphabet

英文索引

ENGLISH INDEX

A

Acting As If There Were No One Near 185
After-Born Should Be Regarded with Awe, The 178
Alighting from the Carriage and Weeping over One's Misdeed 55
All's Fair in Love and War 140
All Men Are Brothers Within the Four Seas 84
Amiable and Easy to Approach 91
As Comfortable As an Old Shoe 91
As Cool As a Cucumber 120
Ashamed of One's Ungainly Appearance 119
At Sixes and Sevens 82
Attacking the Enemy's Mind Is the Most Important of All 131

B

Bagged Fireflies and the Reflected Light of the Snow 270
Basket of Rice, a Gourd Dipper of Drink, A 32
Be the First to Show Concern and the Last to Enjoy Oneself 114
Beard the Lion in His Den 81
Being Pleased with Oneself 148
Better Let Him Who Tied the Bell Untie it 229
Better to Keep Still Than Move 31
Bite Off More Than One Can Chew 48
Blind Man on a Blind Horse, A 151
Bookbinding Snaps Three Times, The 183
Borrowing a Road to Conquer the State of Guo 207
Break into Four Parts, and Each Part Cracks into Five Pieces 82
Breaking Ground Where the God of the Year Presides 81

Bright Mirror Hanging High, A 164

C

Capturing All in One Net 34
Cheek by Jowl 123
Cherishing a Deep-seated Affection 23
Clever Child May Not Distinguish Himself When Grown, A 58
Clever Strategy and Shrewd Tactics 166
Clinging to the Broken and Outworn 162
Coming While in a Joyful Mood 193
Contented Mind Is a Perpetual Feast, A 32
Correct One's Errors and Start Anew 146
Courteous Before Resorting to Force 116
Crowd Assembling Like Crows, A 196
Cutting One's Belly Open to Hide a Pearl 186
Cutting the Mat to Break with an Old Friend 214

D

Decayed Wood and Dirt Wall 122
Disappearing Like the Yellow Crane 159
Dispelling the Clouds and Seeing the Sun 235
Disregarding Moral Principles in Pursuit of Profit 133
Dong Hu's Straight Writing Brush 227
Draped with the Imperial Yellow Robe 208
Drinking More to Cure Drunkenness 80
Drop in the Bucket, A 38
Dying Without Closing One's Eyes 99

E

Each in His Own Place 118
Early Bird Cathes the Worm, The 112
Eight Immortals Cross the Sea, Each One Showing His or Her Special Prowess 37

Enough Books to Make a Pack-Ox Sweat Or to Pile Ceiling-High 92
Establishing Oneself in an Unassailable Position 88
Existing in Name Only 190
Exposing Oneself to Ridicule by the Knowledgeable 226
Eye Cannot See Its Lashes, The 85

F

Far Above the Ordinary 218
Feather Is Not Yet Fully Grown, The 108
Feet Kicking and Eyes Narrowed 243
Fighting a Conflagration with Fire and Controling a Flood with Water 76
First Impressions Are Strongest 113
First Under Heaven, The 61
Fox Dies with Its Face Toward Its Den, A 156
Friendship Between Yang Jiaoai and Zuo Botao 94

G

General Who Fears Not the Loss of His Head, A 259
Glaring Like a Vajra 156
Gradually Entering Blissful Circumstances 234
Grass Stirs When the Wind Blows, The 175
Great Wall, The 211
Green Leaves Make a Shade 237
Greenhorn, A 126
Going into Battle Stripped to the Waist 130
Guest Behind the Curtain, A 47

H

Hacking Through Brambles and Thistles 161
Hang and Xie Breathe the Same Breath 123
Hanging a Book on an Ox Horn 73
Hanging the Camel Up To Be Near to the Whetstone 266

He Who Strikes First Prevails 112
Head and Shoulders Above 218
Head and Tail Correspond with Each Other 165
Head of the Magic Dragon Is Visible and Its Tail Invisible, The 168
Headstrong and Opinionated 202
Heavenly Steed Soaring Across the Skies, A 60
Her Face Is Like a Peach Blossom 43
Hesitate at Making a Chess Move 250
Human Face with the Heart of a Beast, A 45

I

I Am Drunk and Want to Sleep 143
I Would Throw My Lot in with You, Sir, at the Risk of My Life 212
In Name but Not in Reality 103
Intelligible to an Old Woman 98
It Might Be True 200

J

Jade Produced in Lantian 262
Judging a Person Solely by His Appearance 78
Just Coming out of the Thatched Cottage 126

K

Keep Silent and Vanish Without Leaving a Trace Behind 249
Keeping Ah Jiao in a Chamber of Gold 155
Killing the Pig to Teach the Child 204
Killing Three People with Two Peaches 35
Knowing How to Look After Oneself 217

L

Leaving a Name Behind 41
Leaving No Stone Unturned 64
Lengthwise and Breadthwise, Opening and Closing 258

Like Fish or Meat on a Chopping Board 46
Looking at the Heavens Through a Tube 77
Looking Impressive but Lacking Real Worth 221
Loosening One's Tongue and Using Orpiment Freely 176
Lu Meng in the Kingdom of Wu 136

M

Make A Clean Sweep 34
Making A Pretense of Knowledge 216
Making Friends by the Pestle and Mortar 158
Making Impertinent Remarks 89
Man Holding a Sword, The 194
Man with a Set Purpose Will Finally Succeed, A 102
Mentioned in the Same Breath 172
Messenger in Green, The 236
Money Can Move Even the Gods 256
Money Makes the Mare Go 256
Monkey Wearing a Hat, A 124
Mt. Zhongnan Might Be Removed, But the Decision Might Not Be Removed 174
Music Stops the Passing Clouds, The 267
My Theory Has Been Transmitted to the East 132

N

Never Bending in Spite of Repeated Twisting 100
No Mention of Donkey on Three Pages 52
No One Knows in the Dead of the Night 241
No Study, Know Nothing 68
Not Disturbed with a Pretty Woman in One's Lap 139
Not Moved by Honor or Disgrace 264
Not To Be Daunted by Ten Thousand Deaths 209
Not To Be Mentioned in the Same Breath 65
Nothing Is Too Deceitful in War 140

O

Offending Xi Shi the Beauty 187
Old Man at Liqiu, The 248
Once Gone, It Never Comes Back 25
Once It Is Started, Go through with It 27
One Anthill May Cause the Collapse of a Thousand-Li Dyke 54
One Thousand Changes and Ten Thousand Transformations 71
Opening Up a Fresh Look 137

P

Parents Living Under the White Clouds 86
Passing Off Fish Eyes As Pearls 206
Passing One's Own House but Never Going In 228
Passing Through the Hall into the Inner Chamber 72
Power Capable of Drawing Back a Moving Heavenly Body 109
Principle of Kings Wen and Wu Was to Alternate Tension with Relaxation, The 74
Proclaiming One's Might First and Then Demonstrating It 115
Provide for a Rainy Day 163
Pulling Together and Working with One Heart and One Mind 246
Purple Air Comes from the East, The 223
Putting Letters in Hongqiao's Charge 87

Q

Qi-Qi-Ai-Ai 222
Qing-Qing-Wo-Wo 205

R

Rafter-like Writing Brush 53
Reading Ten Lines at a Glance 26
Reinforcing and Counteracting Each Other 173
Remaining Composed in Difficult Situations 120
Rendering Meritorious Service at Mianchi 254

Rice as Precious as Pearls and Firewood as Costly as Cassia 95
Riding the Wind and Breaking the Waves 192
Road is Hard and We Can't Go On (Xing-Bu-De-Ye-Ge-Ge), The 105
Rumors and Gossip Travel Apace 179

S

Satisfied with Old Customs and Outdated Information 97
Scared of His Own Shadow, and Detesting His Own Footprints 184
Seagulls Won't Come Down, The 269
Seeking Benevolence and Acquiring It 128
Selling the Knife to Buy Cattle 245
Serving One's Country Loyally 231
Setting the Whole Room Roaring 257
Sharing Joy and Woe 110
Shilly-shally 250
Shooting Off One's Mouth 176
Short Cut in Mount Zhongnan, A 215
Shortening the Leg of a Crane to Lengthen the Leg of a Wild Duck 260
Single Hair Out of Nine Ox Hides, A 38
Sink or Swim together 110
Sitting on Top of the Mountain to Watch the Tigers Fight 138
Skillful at Dancing with Long Sleeves 147
Sleep on One's Spear Till Daybreak 157
So Lost in Enjoyment As to Forget to Go Home 198
Soaring High into the Clouds 153
Sparing No Pains 64
Speak with One's Tongue in One's Cheek 125
Speaking with One Voice 121
Speed Is What Counts in War 142
Spring Dream, A 29
Standing Gracefully Erect 170
Stitch in Time Saves Nine, A 54
Stopping People's Mouths Is More Difficult Than Damming River 134
Strength Not Equal to the Will 48

Stumbled by a Mound Instead of a Mountain 201
Success After Nine Conversions 40
Sweat Streaming Down and Drenching One's Back 93
Sweeping the Bed Clean in Expectation of a Visitor 213

T

Taking Sole Charge on Any Battlefront 252
Talking and Laughing As If Nothing Had Happened 244
That Fellow Has Made His Name 232
Things in the Medicine Kit 263
Think of Danger While Living in Peace 163
Thinking What a Title or Name Implies 268
Three Nuns and Six Old Women 51
Three Religions and Nine Schools, The 50
Three Sovereigns in One Country 30
To Vomit Out the Heart and Drip Blood 240
Tongshan Mountain Falls in the West and Luo Bronze Bell Responds in the East 238
Too Far Gone To Be Remedied 62
Totally Heartless 106
Turn in One's Grave 99
Turn Over a New Leaf 146
Two Dogs Fight for a Bone, and a Third Runs Away with It 138
Two Sleeves Flapping in the Wind 150

U

Unable to Tell Beans from Wheat 66
Using Others as Mirrors 75
Uttered As If from One Mouth 121

W

Western Paradise 224
Wet Behind the Ears 108

When I See Her, Even I Cannot Help Loving Her 144
Where There's a Will There's a Way 102
Wild Geese Deliver Letters 219
Winged General Has a Bad Fortune, The 180
Withered Tree Brings Forth Flowers, A 171
Wolf and Bei Jackal in Cahoots with Each Other 188
Wolf in Sheep's Skin 45
Words Spoken Are Not from the Heart, The 125
Wrapping a Treasure Up Layer by Layer for Storage 70
Writing a Composition in a Stream 56

Y

Yi Shoots Down Nine Suns 181
You Can't Make a Silk Purse Out of a Sow's Ear 122

Z

Zhi-Hu-Zhe-Ye 59
Zhong Kui Dies of Indignation 195

漢語拼音索引

CHINESE PHONETIC ALPHABET INDEX

A

ān yú gù sú, nì yú jiù wén
安於故俗，溺於舊聞 96

B

bā xiān guò hǎi, gè xiǎn shén tōng
八仙過海，各顯神通 36

bǎi zhé bù náo
百折不撓 100

bái yún qīn shě
白雲親舍 86

bào cán shǒu quē
抱殘守缺 161

bié kāi shēng miàn
別開生面 136

bīng bù yàn zhà
兵不厭詐 140

bīng guì shén sù
兵貴神速 141

bō yún jiàn rì
撥雲見日 234

bù biàn shū mài
不辨菽麥 66

bù kě jiù yào
不可救藥 61

bù kě tóng rì ér yǔ
不可同日而語 64

bù xué wú shù
不學無術 67

bù yí yú lì
不遺餘力 63

C

cháng xiù shàn wǔ
長袖善舞 146

chāo qún jué lún
超群絕倫 217

chéng fēng pò làng
乘風破浪 191

chéng xìng ér lái
乘興而來 192

chì bó shàng zhèn
赤膊上陣 129

chǒng rǔ bù jīng
寵辱不驚 264

chū chū máo lú
初出茅廬 126
chǔ jiù zhī jiāo
杵臼之交 158
chū yán bù xùn
出言不遜 89

D

dà bǐ rú chuán
大筆如椽 52
dǒng hú zhí bǐ
董狐直筆 226
dú dǎng yī miàn
獨當一面 252
duàn hè xù fú
斷鶴續鳧 260
duàn tóu jiāng jūn
斷頭將軍 259

E

èr táo shā sān shì
二桃殺三士 34

F

fēng chuī cǎo dòng
風吹草動 174
fáng mín zhī kǒu, shèn yú fáng chuān
防民之口，甚於防川 134
fēi duǎn liú cháng
飛短流長 178
fēi jiāng shǔ qí
飛將數奇 180
fù zhū hóng qiáo
付諸洪喬 87

G

gǎi guò zì xīn
改過自新 145
gāng bì zì yòng
剛愎自用 202
gè dé qí suǒ
各得其所 118
gē xí duàn jiāo
割蓆斷交 213
gōng xīn wéi shàng
攻心為上 130
gù míng sī yì
顧名思義 267
guò mén bù rù
過門不入 227

H

hàn liú jiā bèi
汗流浹背 93
hàn niú chōng dòng
汗牛充棟 92
hàng xiè yī qì
沆瀣一氣 123
hào zhěng yǐ xiá
好整以暇 120
hōng táng dà xiào
鬨堂大笑 256

hòu shēng kě wèi
後生可畏 177
hú sǐ shǒu qiū
狐死首丘 156
huàng páo jiā shēn
黃袍加身 207
huí tiān zhī lì
回天之力 108

J

jí lè shì jiè
極樂世界 224
jiǎ tú miè guó
假途滅虢 207
jiàn lì wàng yì
見利忘義 132
jiàn rǔ jiā jìng
漸入佳境 233
jiě líng hái xū jì líng rén
解鈴還須繫鈴人 228
jīn gāng nù mù
金剛怒目 155
jīn wū cáng jiāo
金屋藏嬌 154
jìn zhōng bào guó
盡忠報國 230
jiǔ niú yī máo
九牛一毛 38
jiǔ zhuǎn gōng chéng
九轉功成 40
jū ān sī wēi
居安思危 162
jǔ qí bù dìng
舉棋不定 250

K

kū shù shēng huā
枯樹生花 170

L

lān tián shēng yù
藍田生玉 261
láng bèi wéi jiān
狼狽為奸 188
lǎo yù néng jiě
老嫗能解 97
lì bù cóng xīn
力不從心 48
lí qiū zhàng rén
黎丘丈人 247
lì yú bù bài zhī dì
立於不敗之地 88
liǎng xiù qīng fēng
兩袖清風 149
liú lián wàng fǎn
流連忘返 197
lù lì tóng xīn
戮力同心 246
lǜ yè chéng yīn
綠葉成陰 236
lǜ yǐ shì zhě
綠衣使者 235

M

mài dāo mǎi niú
賣刀買牛 245

máng rén xiā mǎ
盲人瞎馬 151

mǐ zhū xīn guì
米珠薪桂 95

miǎn chí zhī gōng
澠池之功 253

míng jìng gāo xuán
明鏡高懸 163

mò tuí yú shān, ér tuí yú dié
莫蹪於山，而蹪於垤 200

mò xū yǒu
莫須有 198

mù bù jiàn jié
目不見睫 85

mù hóu ér guàn
沐猴而冠 124

mù yè wú zhī
暮夜無知 240

N

nán shān kě yí, pàn bù kě yáo
南山可移，判不可搖 173

náng yíng yìng xuě
囊螢映雪 269

niú jiǎo guà shū
牛角掛書 73

O

ōu niǎo bù xià
鷗鳥不下 268

ōu xīn lì xuè
嘔心瀝血 239

P

páng ruò wú rén
旁若無人 185

pī jīng zhǎn jí
披荊斬棘 160

píng yì jìn rén
平易近人 90

pōu fù cǎng zhū
剖腹藏珠 186

pū shù mí lí
撲朔迷離 242

Q

qī qī āi āi
期期艾艾 221

qì shā zhōng kuí
氣殺鍾馗 194

qiān biàn wàn huà
千變萬化 70

qián kě tōng shén
錢可通神 255

qiān lǐ zhī dī, kuì yú yǐ xué
千里之堤，潰於蟻穴 53

qiǎng bù zhī yǐ wéi zhī
強不知以為知 215

qīng qīng wǒ wǒ
卿卿我我 204
qīng yún zhí shàng
青雲直上 152
qiú rén dé rén
求仁得仁 128
quán wú xīn gán
全無心肝 105

R

rén miàn shòu xīn
人面獸心 44
rén miàn táo huā
人面桃花 42
rén sǐ liú míng
人死留名 41
rén wéi dāo zǔ, wǒ wéi yú ròu
人為刀俎，我為魚肉 45
rú chū yī kǒu
如出一口 121
rù mù zhī bīn
入幕之賓 46

S

sān gū liù pó
三姑六婆 50
sān jiào jiǔ liú
三教九流 49
sān zhǐ wú lǘ
三紙無驢 51
sǎo tà yǐ yíng
掃榻以迎 212
shā zhì jiào zǐ
殺彘教子 203
shàn zì wéi móu
善自為謀 216
shě mìng péi jūn zǐ
捨命陪君子 211
shén jī miào suàn
神機妙算 166
shén lóng jiàn shǒu bù jiàn wěi
神龍見首不見尾 168
shēng táng rù shì
升堂入室 72
shí xí zhēn cáng
什襲珍藏 69
shǒu wěi xiāng yìng
首尾相應 165
shù zǐ chéng míng
豎子成名 231
sǐ bù míng mù
死不瞑目 98
sì fēn wǔ liè
四分五裂 82
sì hǎi zhī nèi jiē xiōng dì
四海之內皆兄弟 83

T

tài suì tóu shàng dòng tǔ
太歲頭上動土 81

tán xiào zì ruò
談笑自若 243
táng tū xī shī
唐突西施 187
tiān mǎ xíng kōng
天馬行空 59
tiān xià dì yī
天下第一 60
tíng tíng yù lì
亭亭玉立 169
tóng gān gòng kǔ
同甘共苦 109
tóng shān xī bēng, luò zhōng dōng yìng
銅山西崩，洛鐘東應 238
tú yǒu xū míng
徒有虛名 189

W

wàn lǐ cháng chéng
萬里長城 210
wàn sǐ bù cí
萬死不辭 208
wéi biān sān jué
韋編三絕 183
wèi yǐng wù jī
畏影惡跡 184
wén wǔ zhī dào, yī zhāng yī chí
文武之道，一張一弛 74
wǒ jiàn yóu lián
我見猶憐 144
wǒ zuì yù mián
我醉欲眠 143
wú dào dōng yǐ
吾道東矣 131
wū hé zhī zhòng
烏合之眾 196
wú xià ā méng
吳下阿蒙 135

X

xià bǐ chéng zhāng
下筆成章 55
xià chē qì zuì
下車泣罪 54
xiān lǐ hòu bīng
先禮後兵 116
xiān rù wéi zhǔ
先入為主 112
xiān shēng hòu shí
先聲後實 115
xiān xià shǒu wéi qiáng
先下手為強 111
xiān yōu hòu lè
先憂後樂 114
xiǎng è xíng yǔn
響遏行雲 266
xiāng shēng xiāng kè
相生相克 172
xiāng tí bìng lùn
相提並論 171

xiāo shēng nì jī
銷聲匿跡 248
xiǎo shí liǎo liǎo, dà wéi bì jiā
小時了了，大未必佳 57
xìn kǒu cí huáng
信口雌黃 176
xíng bù dé yě gē gē
行不得也哥哥 104
xiǔ mù fèn qiáng
朽木糞牆 122
xū yǒu qí biǎo
虛有其表 220
xuán tuó jiù shí
懸駝就石 265

Y

yán bù yóu zhōng
言不由衷 125
yàn zú chuán shū
雁足傳書 219
yáng zuǒ zhī jiāo
羊左之交 94
yào lóng zhōng wù
藥籠中物 263
yǎo rú huáng hè
杳如黃鶴 159
yī bù zuò, èr bù xiū
一不做，二不休 26
yī cháng chūn mèng
一場春夢 28
yī dān yī piáo
一簞一瓢 31
yī dòng bù rú yī jìng
一動不如一靜 30
yǐ guǎn kuī tiān
以管窺天 77
yì guó sān gōng
一國三公 29
yǐ huǒ jiù huǒ, yǐ shuǐ jiù shuǐ
以火救火，以水救水 76
yǐ jiǔ jiě chéng
以酒解酲 80
yǐ mào qǔ rén
以貌取人 78
yú mù hùn zhū
魚目混珠 205
yī mù shí háng
一目十行 25
yī qù bù fù fǎn
一去不復返 24
yǐ rén wéi jiàn
以人為鑒 75
yì shè jiǔ rì
羿射九日 181
yī wǎng dǎ jìn
一網打盡 33
yī wǎng qíng shēn
一 往 情 深 23
yí xiào dà fāng
貽笑大方 225

yǒu míng wú shí
有名無實 103
yǒu zhì zhě shì jìng chéng
有志者事竟成 102
yǔ máo wèi fēng
羽毛未豐 107

Z

zhān zhān zì xǐ
沾沾自喜 148
zhěn gē dài dàn
枕戈待旦 157
zhī hū zhě yě
之乎者也 58
zhōng nán jié jìng
終南捷徑 214
zhuō dāo rén
捉刀人 193
zì cán xíng huì
自慚形穢 119
zǐ qì dōng lái
紫氣東來 222
zòng héng bǎi hé
縱橫捭闔 257
zuò huái bù luàn
坐懷不亂 138
zuò shān guān hǔ dòu
坐山觀虎鬥 137

引用書目
BIBLIOGRAPHY

Amitabha Sutra
Anecdotes from Tang Dynasty Poetry
Anecdotes of the Kaiyuan and Tianbao Reigns
Anecdotes of the States
Anecdotes of the Warring States
Anecdotes of Yan Zi
Anecdotes Past and Present
Biographies of Virtuous Women
Book of Bao Pu Zi, The
Book of Han Fei Zi, The
Book of Huai Nan Zi, The
Book of Lie Zi, The
Book of Mencius, The
Book of Mo Zi, The
Book of Paying Tribute to Heaven
Book of Rites, The
Book of Songs, The
Book of Sun Zi, The
Book of the Song Dynasty
Book of the Song and Qi Dynasties , The
Book of Xun Zi, The
Book of Zhuang Zi, The
Brief Biography of Li Changji, A
Collection of Paintings
Combining Three Taoist Principles in One
Compendium of Materia Medica
Confucian Analects
Discourses of Lü Buwei, The
Discourses Weighted in the Balance
Eight Immortals' Voyage to the East, The

Entering the Capital
Epitaph for Lu Chun
Essays by Wu Zixu
Family Admonitions of the Yans
Garden of Stories, The
Handwritten Records on the Eastern Chamber
History As a Mirror
History of the Han Dynasty
History of the Jin Dynasty
History of the Later Han Dynasty
History of the Liang Dynasty
History of the Northern Dynasties
History of the Northern Qi Dynasty
History of the Song Dynasty
History of the Southern Dynasties
History of the Southern Qi Dynasty
History of the Three Kingdoms
Letters to Ren An
Miscellaneous Notes of the Western Capital
Miscellany of the Youyang Mountains
Narrative Poems
New Book of the South
New History of the Five Dynasties
New History of the Tang Dynasty
New Social Anecdotes
Night Talks at Cool Studio
Notes by Zhang Duanyi
Notes by Zhao Lingzhi
Notes by Zhao Yanwei
Notes on the Investigation of Things
Notes Taken During Intervals of Ploughing in South Village
Ode to Mu Lan
Old History of the Tang Dynasty
Poetry of Sa Tianxi
Pointing to the Moon

Random Notes by Wen Ying
Random Notes of Emperor Minghuang
Random Talks in Leisure Time
Records After Returning to the Farm
Records of Dragons
Records of Jinyang
Records of the Historian
Stories Ancient and Modern
Stories Compiled in the Taiping Period
Story of Emperor Wudi of the Han Dynasty
Strange Tales
Strange Tales from the Make-Do Studio
Sutra of One Hundred Parables
Taiping Imperial Encyclopedia
Tales of the Three Kingdoms
Tale of Yue Fei, A
Tale of Zhong Kui Catching Ghosts, A
Travel Notes on Yueyang Tower
Trifling Words of Northern Dream
Zuo Qiuming's Chronicles

中國歷史年代簡表

A CHRONOLOGY OF CHINESE DYNASTIES

夏		約公元前 21 世紀——公元前 17 世紀
商		約公元前 17 世紀——公元前 11 世紀
周		約公元前 11 世紀——公元前 256 年
西周		約公元前 11 世紀——公元前 771 年
東周		公元前 770 年——公元前 256 年
	春秋	公元前 770 年——公元前 476 年
	戰國	公元前 475 年——公元前 221 年
秦		公元前 221 年——公元前 206 年
漢		公元前 206 年——公元 220 年
西漢		公元前 206 年——公元 25 年
東漢		公元 25 年——公元 220 年
三國		公元 220 年——公元 280 年
魏		公元 220 年——公元 265 年
蜀		公元 221 年——公元 263 年
吳		公元 222 年——公元 280 年
晉		公元 265 年——公元 420 年
西晉		公元 265 年——公元 317 年
東晉		公元 317 年——公元 420 年
南北朝		公元 420 年——公元 589 年
南朝		公元 420 年——公元 589 年
	宋	公元 420 年——公元 479 年
	齊	公元 479 年——公元 502 年
	梁	公元 502 年——公元 557 年

	陳	公元557年——公元589年
北朝		公元386年——公元581年
	北魏	公元386年——公元534年
	東魏	公元534年——公元550年
	西魏	公元535年——公元556年
	北齊	公元550年——公元577年
	北周	公元557年——公元581年
隋		公元581年——公元619年
唐		公元618年——公元907年
五代		公元907年——公元960年
宋		公元960年——公元1279年
北宋		公元960年——公元1127年
南宋		公元1127年——公元1279年
遼		公元907年——公元1125年
金		公元1115年——公元1234年
元		公元1206年——公元1368年
明		公元1368年——公元1644年
清		公元1616年——公元1911年

Xia	c. 21st century — 17th century B.C.
Shang	c. 17th century — 11th century B.C.
Zhou	c. 11th century — 256 B.C.
Western Zhou	c. 11th century — 771 B.C.
Eastern Zhou	770 — 256 B.C.
Spring and Autumn Period	770 — 476 B.C.
Warring States Period	475 — 221 B.C.
Qin	221 — 206 B.C.
Han	206 B.C. — A.D. 220
Western Han	206 B.C. — A.D. 25
Eastern Han	25 — 220
Three Kingdoms	220 — 280
Wei	220 — 265
Shu	221 — 263
Wu	222 — 280
Jin	265 — 420
Western Jin	265 — 317
Eastern Jin	317 — 420
Southern and Northern Dynasties	420 — 589
Southern Dynasties	420 — 589
Song	420 — 479
Qi	479 — 502
Liang	502 — 557
Chen	557 — 589
Northern Dynasties	386 — 581
Northern Wei	386 — 534
Eastern Wei	534 — 550
Western Wei	535 — 556
Northern Qi	550 — 577
Northern Zhou	557 — 581
Sui	581 — 619

Tang	618 — 907
Five Dynasties	907 — 960
Song	960 — 1279
Northern Song	960 — 1127
Southern Song	1127 — 1279
Liao	907— 1125
Kin	1115 — 1234
Yuan	1206 — 1368
Ming	1368 — 1644
Qing	1616 — 1911

漢語拼音發音指南

GUIDE TO CHINESE PHONETIC ALPHABET

請注意以下幾點：

q 發英文中的 *ch* 聲音，如 cheer, chimney, chin。

x 發英文中的 *sh* 聲音，如 she, shell, shoe。

z 發英文中的 *ds* 聲音，如 reads, records, seeds。

c 發英文中的 *ts* 聲音，如 dots, products, students。

*　*　*　*

中國普通話裡有四種聲調，每個字都有一種聲調，即音調的升降。如：

第一聲（ˉ），高而平；

第二聲（ˊ），升；

第三聲（ˇ），由降而升；

第四聲（ˋ），降。

聲調符號標在主要母音上邊，如這個主要母音是 i，則不標。

聲調在漢語中很重要，同音的字由於聲調不同，字義也就不同。如：

mā	má	mǎ	mà
媽	麻	馬	罵

yī	yí	yǐ	yì
一	移	椅	譯

Watch out for these letters:

q sounds like *ch* in "cheer", "chimney", "chin".

x sounds like *sh* in "she", "shell", "shoe".

z sounds like the final *ds* in "reads", "records", "seeds".

c sounds like the final *ts* in "dots", "products", "students".

*** *** ***

Every Chinese character has a tone which is actually the contour of the rise or fall in pitch during pronunciation. There are four tones in *putonghua* (common speech), shown by the following marks:

ˉ 1st tone, high and level;

ˊ 2nd tone, rising;

ˇ 3rd tone, falling-rising; and

ˋ 4th tone, falling.

The tone mark is placed above the main vowel; when the main vowel is "i", the dot is omitted.

The tones are extremely important. Characters which have the same sound (that is, are spelled the same way in the phonetic alphabet) may have different meanings, and this is indicated by the tone. For example:

mā	má	mǎ	mà
mother	hemp	horse	scold
yī	yí	yǐ	yì
one	move	chair	translate

Chinese Phonetic Alphabet	International Phonetic Alphabet	Chinese Phonetic Alphabet	International Phonetic Alphabet	Chinese Phonetic Alphabet	International Phonetic Alphabet	Chinese Phonetic Alphabet.	International phonetic Alphabet
b	[p]	s	[s]	ê	[ɛ]	ian	[ian]
p	[p‘]	zh	[tʂ]	er	[ər]	in	[in]
m	[m]	ch	[tʂ ’]			iang	[iaŋ]
f	[f]	sh	[ʂ]	ai	[ai]	ing	[iŋ]
d	[t]	r	[ʐ]	ei	[ei]	iong	[yŋ]
t	[t‘]			ao	[au]	ua	[ua]
n	[n]	y	[i]	ou	[əu]	uo	[uə]
l	[l]	w	[w]	an	[an]	uai	[uai]
g	[k]			en	[ən]	ui, uei	[uei]
k	[k‘]	a	[a]	ang	[aŋ]	uan	[uan]
h	[x]	o	[o]	eng	[əŋ]	un, uen	[uən]
j	[tɕ]	e	[ə]	ong	[uŋ]	uang	[uaŋ]
q	[tɕ ‘]	i	[i]	ia	[ia]	ue	[yɛ]
x	[ɕ]	u	[u]	ie	[iɛ]	uan	[yan]
z	[ts]	u	[y]	iao	[iau]	un	[yn]
c	[ts‘]	-1	[ɿ] [ʅ]*	iu, iou	[iəu]		

[l] used after z,c,s; [ʅ] used after zh, ch, sh, r.

Best Chinese Idioms (Volume 1)

中國成語選粹

Editor: Situ Tan

Translators: Zhao Shuhan   Tang Bowen

編者：司徒談

英譯者：趙書漢　　湯博文

The present book contains 206 Chinese idioms which are in common use and behind each of which there is a story or an anecdote. Generally speaking, the stories and anecdotes are based on the original versions in classical Chinese but, where necessary, abridgement and modifications are made and brief descriptions of their backgrounds given. Many of the Chinese idioms are accompanied by English equivalents. Chinese phonetic spelling(*pinyin*) is given to each title, and for readers who are not familiar with this system the appendix "key to Chinese Phonetic Alphabet" at the end of the book may prove useful.

本書選編了常用的和有故事性的成語二百零六條。在介紹成語故事時，一般按照古文直譯，但有的地方也做了一些刪節和修飾，增加了一點背景材料。許多中國成語並列有意義相近的英語成語。

"目次"按字首筆劃順序排列。書末附有按漢語拼音字母排列的條目索引。

Paperback　　21 × 14 cm 352 pp.　　67 illus.

Bilingual Chinese-English

HF-51-P　　ISBN 962-238-033-6　　HK$52

Best Chinese Idioms (Volume 2)

中國成語選粹續篇

Editor: Situ Tan
Translator: Tang Bowen
編者：司徒談
英譯者：湯博文

The present book, a continuation of the Best Chinese Idioms contains 203 Chinese idioms which are in common used and behind each of which there is also a story of an anecdote.

本書為《中國成語選粹》的續集，共收錄常用的和有故事性的成語二百零三條。

Paperback　　*21 × 14 cm 354 pp.*　　*50 illus.*
Bilingual Chinese-English
HF-71-P　　*ISBN 962-238-093-X*　　*HK$52*